Life Style Daily

true facts that sound like bullshit

Table of Contents

Chapter 1: The Animal Kingdom ....

    Section: Animal Intelligence ....

    Section: Extreme Life ....

    Section: Social Behaviors ....

    Section: Myths About Animals ....

    Section: Strange Physical Traits ....

Chapter 2: The Human Body ....

    Section: Phenomena of the Human Body ....

    Section: Fascinating Facts About the Brain ....

    Section: Senses – More Than Five ....

    Section: Genetic Superpowers ....

    Section: Unusual Human Behaviors ....

Chapter 3: Space and Astronomy ....

    Section: Planets and Stars ....

    Section: Black Holes and Their Mysteries ....

    Section: Light Phenomena ....

    Section: Life Beyond Earth ....

    Section: Planetary Motions and Mysterious Phenomena ....

Chapter 4: Plants and Ecology ....

    Section: Carnivorous Plants that Feed on Animals ....

    Section: Plant Defense Mechanisms ....

    Section: Extreme Habitats ....

    Section: The Role of Plants in Ecosystems ....

    Section: Plants That Predict the Weather ....

Chapter 5: Culture and History 37
Section: Strange Historical Customs 37
Section: Phenomena of Human Communities 38
Section: Mysterious Figures and Their Stories 40
Section: Ancient Beliefs and Facts 42
Section: Innovations That Changed the World 43

Chapter 6: Technology and Inventions 46
Section: Accidental Inventions 46
Section: Unusual Uses of Everyday Items 47
Section: Technologies That Surpass Our Understanding 49
Section: Mistakes That Led to Discoveries 50
Section: Lost Inventions 52

Chapter 7: Nature and Geology 54
Section: Volcanic Phenomena 54
Section: Mysterious Lakes and Rivers 55
Section: Extraordinary Mountains and Rock Formations 57
Section: Earth as a Living Organism 58
Section: The Rock Cycle 60

Section 8: Food Curiosities 62
Section: Foods with Surprising Flavors 62
Section: Food in World Cultures 63
Section: History of Culinary Customs 65
Section: Culinary Art of Past Eras 66
Section: Animals in Human Cuisine 68

Chapter 9: The World of Science 71

    Section: The Physics of Everyday Life 71

    Section: Biology We Never Knew 72

    Section: The Chemical Mysteries 74

    Section: Geometry and Mathematics in Everyday Life 76

    Section: Discoveries That Will Shape the Future 77

Chapter 10: Everyday Life 80

    Section: Strange Customs and Superstitions 80

    Section: Rituals That Survive to This Day 81

    Section: Everyday Objects 83

    Section: Human Labor and Other Professions 85

    Section: Facts About Our Daily Lives 86

Summary of the Book 89

All rights are reserved 2024 by Life Style Daily. No part of this publication may be reproduced, stored in a retrieval system or transmitted in any form or by any means, electronic, mechanical, photocopying, recording or otherwise, without prior permission.

Welcome to a world of facts that sound like made-up stories but are 100% true! True Facts That Sound Like Bull#t is a book that surprises on every page, uncovering incredible tidbits from all areas of life. How many times have you heard something that seemed too bizarre to be real? That's exactly the kind of fact we've gathered here—stories so extraordinary they might seem unbelievable, yet they're grounded in reality.

This book isn't just a random collection of trivia. Each chapter is carefully crafted to take you on a journey through different realms of our reality: from the fascinating abilities of animals and the mysteries of space, to unique human behaviors and unexpected scientific discoveries. Here, you'll find answers to questions you may have never thought to ask, but that are sure to captivate you entirely.

Why did we write this? Because life and our world are more astonishing than any fiction. Sometimes the truth seems impossible to believe, yet it's documented and backed by facts. This book was created to inspire, entertain, and—let's be honest—provide plenty of conversation starters that are sure to amaze your friends.

So, get ready to laugh, marvel, and be genuinely wowed. In the world of True Facts That Sound Like Bull#t, the line between the possible and the unbelievable simply doesn't exist.

Chapter 1: The Animal Kingdom

Section: Animal Intelligence

Octopuses Can Use Tools – Some octopuses gather coconut shells to create portable "armor."

Crows Recognize Human Faces – They can remember people who harmed or helped them, even years later.

Dolphins Give Themselves "Names" – They produce unique sounds that function as names, recognized by other dolphins.

Elephants Mourn Their Dead – They visit places where another elephant has died and "grieve" its passing.

Chimpanzees Learn from Each Other – They use simple tools, like sticks to fish for termites, and pass these techniques down through generations.

Parrots Understand the Concept of Numbers – The African grey parrot, Alex, could distinguish colors, shapes, and count objects.

Ants Wage "Wars" Against Other Colonies – They organize coordinated attacks and have complex social structures.

Woodpeckers are the "Doctors" of the Forest – They remember the exact locations of trees infested by insects and return to "treat" them.

Bees Communicate Through "Dances" – They inform other bees about food locations using precise movements.

Cows Have Best Friends – They form friendships with other cows and feel stressed when separated from them.

Owls Create "Mimic" Calls – They imitate other animals to lure in prey.

Wolves Have a Complex Communication System – They use body language, howling, and other sounds depending on the situation.

Dolphins Know Basic "Medicine" – They've been seen rubbing wounds on certain corals with antibacterial properties.

7

Cats "Manipulate" Humans Through Meowing – They produce a special tone of meow that triggers a caregiving response in people.

Spiders Build "Social Networks" – Some species live in large colonies and hunt prey collectively.

Cockatoos Can Dance to a Beat – The cockatoo Snowball showed an ability to synchronize movements with music.

Woodpeckers "Decorate" Their Nests – They place colorful objects around their nesting areas, which may be a form of decorating.

Octopuses Learn by Watching – They can imitate the behaviors of other octopuses, even without prior experience.

Orcas Can "Plan Attacks" – They coordinate group actions to push ice with a seal on it into the water.

Chickens Have Their Own "Language" – They produce around 30 different communicative sounds, each with specific meanings, like alarms for predators.

Section: Extreme Life

Tardigrades Survive Almost Anything – These microscopic creatures can endure outer space, extreme temperatures, and survive without water for years.

Turtles That Breathe Through Their Tails – Some freshwater turtles can absorb oxygen through openings in their tails, allowing them to stay underwater for extended periods.

Emperor Penguins Withstand Extreme Cold – These birds endure temperatures as low as -60°C while wintering in Antarctica.

Deep-Sea Shrimp Endure Massive Pressure – They live at depths where pressure can be up to 1,000 times greater than at the surface.

Frogs Freeze Themselves for Winter – The wood frog can completely freeze and survive until spring, when it thaws out.

Fleas Survive High Altitudes – Though tiny, they withstand extreme altitude changes, enabling them to survive in diverse environments.

Whales Dive to Extreme Depths – Sperm whales dive over 2 kilometers deep to hunt for squid.

Polar Sharks in Arctic Waters – These sharks inhabit frigid Arctic waters and can live up to 400 years thanks to a slow metabolism.

Salmonid Fish Live in Super Cold Waters – They survive in below-freezing waters thanks to special anti-freeze proteins.

Volcano-Dwelling Spiders – Some spider species can survive on hot volcanic terrain where temperatures are too high for most creatures.

Desert Plants Attract Extreme Animals – Scorpions and snakes are adapted to desert life, enduring long stretches without water.

Alligators Survive in Ice – In some regions, alligators freeze themselves in winter with only their nostrils poking above the ice.

Sea Turtles Migrate Thousands of Miles – Some sea turtles migrate up to 20,000 kilometers over their lifetimes.

Lungfish Survive Droughts – These fish bury themselves in mud during dry seasons and can live without water for several months.

Extremophile Mollusks – They thrive in boiling hot springs and near hydrothermal vents, where water temperatures reach boiling.

Arctic Foxes – With fur that protects them even in -70°C temperatures, they are well adapted to Arctic life.

King Crabs in Icy Waters – Adapted to very low temperatures, they can hunt and survive on the cold ocean floor.

Amazonian Frogs Adapted to Toxic Environments – They thrive in areas with toxic plants and have adapted to eat insects that other animals avoid.

Birds Flying Across the Himalayas – Tibetan geese fly at altitudes above 7,000 meters, tolerating low oxygen levels.

Arctic Worms – Nematodes that inhabit the icy Arctic regions are adapted to survive in extreme cold.

Section: Social Behaviors

Dolphins Help Injured Group Members – When a dolphin is injured or sick, other dolphins in the group support it to help it breathe.

Ants Care for Their Wounded – When an ant is injured in battle, other ants bring it back to the nest and care for it.

Elephants "Mourn" Their Dead – Elephants sometimes return to the site where a herd member has died and stand there silently.

Lions Form Social Structures in Prides – Each lion has a specific role, and the females work together to care for the young.

Wolves Have a Social Hierarchy – Each wolf pack has a strict hierarchy, with an alpha male and female leading the group.

Meerkats Take Turns as Lookouts – In meerkat groups, one individual stands guard to alert the group of approaching danger.

Gorillas Have Complex Family Relationships – The alpha male, or silverback, protects and leads the group, earning respect from its members.

Emperor Penguins Share Parenting Duties – Males incubate the eggs while females go on long trips to find food.

Bonobos Share Food – Bonobos are known for sharing food with group members, strengthening social bonds.

Orcas Hunt in Coordinated Groups – They cooperate to push prey into the water, often using complex hunting strategies.

Vampire Bats Share Blood with Friends – When a bat doesn't find food, other bats share their meal with it.

Starlings Form Murmurations – Flying in coordinated groups protects them from predators and helps conserve energy.

Cows Bond with Specific Individuals – They form friendships within the herd, spending more time with chosen "friends."

Ducks and Geese Have Family Structures – They often return to the same nesting areas to reconnect with family groups.

Starlings Cooperate to Defend Nests – They form complex flight patterns to deter predators like hawks and falcons.

Bees Decide on a New Nest Together – Before establishing a new colony, they send out scouts who "vote" on the best location.

Chimpanzees Show Affection – They groom each other and play together, which strengthens bonds within the group.

Crows Form "Alliances" – In challenging situations, they join forces to solve problems or defend against threats.

Coral Reef Fish Live in "Communities" – They form groups that cooperate in defense against predators.

Bison Stay in Herds for Protection – They live in large groups, which helps them defend against predators like wolves.

Section: Myths About Animals

Bats Are Blind – In reality, bats have good eyesight and also use echolocation to navigate in the dark.

Camels Store Water in Their Humps – Camel humps store fat, not water; they actually retain water in their bloodstream.

Lemmings Commit Mass Suicide – This myth spread due to a Disney film; in truth, large-scale deaths occur because of the challenges of migration.

Dogs See Only in Black and White – Dogs have limited color vision but can see colors like yellow and blue.

Goldfish Have a Three-Second Memory – Studies show goldfish can remember for weeks or even months.

Ostriches Bury Their Heads in the Sand When Scared – Ostriches don't bury their heads: they kneel to check on their eggs.

Spiders Eat Their Webs Daily – Most spiders rebuild their webs but don't consume them regularly.

Sharks Never Sleep – Sharks do sleep, often by resting one hemisphere of their brain at a time.

Electric Eels Can Kill a Human with a Shock – While electric eels have strong impulses, they're unlikely to kill; their shocks are more paralyzing.

Hamsters Hibernate in Winter – Only some hamster species hibernate; many remain active year-round.

Dogs Can Safely Eat Bones – Not all bones are safe for dogs, especially cooked ones, which can splinter and be dangerous.

Owls Are Wise – While owls are skilled hunters, their brains are less developed compared to other birds of prey.

Frogs Can Only Live in Water – Many frog species are adapted to life on land and spend most of their lives there.

Snakes Hypnotize Their Prey – Snakes don't have hypnotic powers; prey often freezes due to fear.

Swans Mate for Life – Swans are known for monogamy but sometimes change partners during their lifetimes.

Toads Cause Warts – Warts are caused by viruses, not contact with toads.

Goats Eat Everything – Goats are actually picky; they explore new things but eat only what they deem suitable.

Stingrays Attack People Without Reason – Stingrays generally attack only in self-defense, such as when someone steps on them.

Cats Are Loners – Cats can form strong social bonds and friendships with other cats and people.

Toads Don't Swim – Many toads spend time in water, though they generally prefer drier habitats.

Section: Strange Physical Traits

Chameleons Can Move Their Eyes Independently – Each eye can move separately, allowing chameleons to see in two different directions at once.

Sharks Have a "Sixth Sense" for Detecting Electricity – Thanks to their ampullae of Lorenzini, sharks can sense electrical signals emitted by other animals.

Frogs Breathe Through Their Skin – Frog skin is permeable to gases, enabling them to breathe even underwater.

Mountain Goat Eyes Glow Gold in Winter – Their eyes change color to improve night vision in the low light of winter nights.

Woodpeckers' Tongues Wrap Around Their Skulls – A woodpecker's tongue is longer than its head and wraps around the skull to protect its brain during pecking.

Lizards Can Detach Their Tails – When threatened, many lizards can drop their tail, which keeps moving to distract predators.

Ants Can Lift Multiple Times Their Weight – Depending on the species, ants can carry 10 to 50 times their body weight.

Glass Frogs Are Almost Transparent – Species like the glass frog have nearly see-through skin, allowing visibility of their internal organs.

A Chameleon's Tongue is Longer Than Its Body – This allows them to catch insects from a distance, launching their tongue at lightning speed.

Kiwi Birds Have Nostrils at the End of Their Beaks – Kiwi are the only birds with nostrils at the tip of their beak, helping them sense food in the soil.

Fish that Pollinate Like Bees – Some fish species help pollinate aquatic plants, carrying pollen on their bodies.

Geckos Can Walk on Walls – Their feet are covered with millions of microscopic hairs that allow them to stick to surfaces like Velcro.

Pistol Shrimp Create Shockwaves – They snap their claws with such force that they generate imploding bubbles, producing sound waves.

Orb-Weaving Spiders Have "Golden Silk" – This silk is not only strong but also has a golden hue, aiding in camouflage.

Seals Have Specialized Senses in Their Whiskers – Seals detect water movements through sensitive whiskers, aiding in hunting.

Salamanders Have Extremely Thin Skin – Salamanders breathe through their skin, which is so thin it must stay moist to absorb oxygen.

Porcupine Quills Act Like Needles – Porcupine quills are hollow, making them lightweight yet sharp for effective defense.

A Snail's Heart is in Its Foot – A snail's circulatory system is located near its foot, which helps with circulation throughout its body.

Pufferfish Eyes Are Telescopic – They can move each eye independently, allowing them to detect threats from multiple angles.

Elephant Trunks Help Them Cool Off – Elephants use their trunks to regulate temperature by cooling the blood vessels within.

Chapter 2: The Human Body

Section: Phenomena of the Human Body

The Stomach Digests Itself but Constantly Renews – The stomach lining is coated in a special mucus that protects it from its own acid, and the cells renew every few days.

The Brain Generates Enough Energy to Power a Light Bulb – The flow of electrical impulses in the brain is intense enough to power a 10-watt bulb.

Bones Are Five Times Stronger Than Steel – Bone structure makes it extremely durable yet relatively light.

Skin Is the Largest Organ – In an average adult, the skin covers about 2 square meters.

Eyes Can Differentiate About 10 Million Colors – Human vision is remarkably sensitive to colors and shades, though limited to the visible spectrum.

Human Hair Is Practically Indestructible – Apart from burning, hair is resistant to many chemical and biological factors.

The Human Heart Beats an Average of 100,000 Times a Day – Every day, the heart pumps about 2,000 gallons (7,570 liters) of blood.

The Stomach Can Dissolve Steel Blades – Hydrochloric acid in the stomach is strong enough to theoretically dissolve steel, although the body quickly expels such objects.

Lungs Have a Surface Area of About 750 Square Feet (70 m²) – Thanks to the alveoli, the lungs provide a vast surface for gas exchange.

The Nose Can Remember About 50,000 Scents – Our sense of smell is highly developed and can trigger vivid memories.

Humans Have a Unique Tongue Print – Just like fingerprints, each person has a unique tongue print.

Our Body Produces Around 600,000 Skin Cells Every Hour – We shed close to a million skin cells daily, which are continuously replaced.

Bones Are Constantly Renewed – The human skeleton is completely renewed approximately every ten years through a continuous process of breakdown and rebuilding.

Saliva Contains Natural Painkillers – Human saliva includes opiorphin, which acts as a natural painkiller.

The Human Brain Works Faster Than a Supercomputer – While processing information differently, the human brain is incredibly efficient at parallel processing.

Most Household Dust Is Dead Skin – Up to 70-80% of dust in homes consists of dead skin cells.

Blood Vessels Can Stretch 62,000 Miles (100,000 km) – The total length of blood vessels in an adult is enough to circle the Earth twice.

A Child's Eyes Fully Develop by Age Six – A newborn's vision is blurry, but it sharpens over time, reaching full capability around age six.

The Brain Uses 20% of the Body's Energy – Though only 2% of body mass, it requires significant energy for optimal function.

The Human Body Emits Light – We emit infrared light, invisible to the eye, which can be captured by special cameras.

Section: Fascinating Facts About the Brain

The Brain is 75% Water – Proper hydration is essential for its optimal function.

The Human Brain Can Form Up to 1 Million Synaptic Connections Per Second – This process is especially intense during childhood.

The Average Brain Generates About 50,000 Thoughts Per Day – Most of these thoughts are routine, and some may even be negative.

The Brain Itself Feels No Pain – While it has pain receptors in the surrounding membranes, the brain itself lacks pain receptors.

The Human Brain Reaches Full Size Around Age 18 but Develops Until Age 25 – The areas responsible for emotions and decision-making mature last.

Memory Capacity is Theoretically Unlimited – The brain can store massive amounts of information, though effectiveness depends on learning methods.

The Brain Works Faster Than a Supercomputer – In terms of processing power and connections, it outpaces even the most advanced computers.

The Average Brain Weighs About 3 Pounds (1.4 kg) – It is heavier than the brains of other primates, partly accounting for higher intelligence.

The Brain Uses 20% of the Body's Energy – Although it makes up only 2% of body mass, it consumes one-fifth of the body's energy.

Learning Physically Changes the Brain – Creating new neural connections alters its structure and organization.

Sleep is Essential for "Cleansing" the Brain – During sleep, the brain clears toxins accumulated throughout the day.

The Brain is More Active at Night than During the Day – While we sleep, it intensively processes and consolidates information.

The Brain Doesn't Distinguish Between Imagination and Reality – Vivid imagination can trigger responses similar to those caused by real experiences.

Chronic Stress Can Shrink the Brain – Prolonged stress reduces the size of the hippocampus, essential for memory and learning.

The Left Brain Controls the Right Side of the Body, and Vice Versa – Each hemisphere of the brain controls the opposite side of the body.

The Brain Can Form New Neurons Throughout Life – Neurogenesis, the creation of new neurons, is possible, particularly in areas related to memory.

The Brain Uses Less Energy for Automatic Tasks – Once a task becomes routine, the brain requires less energy, improving efficiency.

The Brain Has "Sensory Maps" – Each part of the body has a corresponding area in the brain for processing sensory input.

The Brain is Plastic – It can adjust its structure and functions to new challenges, key to learning and adaptation.

The Brain is Active Even During Deep Sleep – Even in deep sleep, the brain remains active, regulating vital functions and processing information

Section: Senses – More Than Five

Sense of Balance (Proprioception) – This allows us to maintain balance and body orientation in space, thanks to the vestibular system in the inner ear.

Sense of Temperature (Thermoreception) – Skin has receptors that detect temperature changes, helping us feel warmth and cold.

Sense of Pain (Nociception) – Pain receptors throughout the body alert us to injuries and potential dangers.

Sense of Spatial Orientation – Helps us determine the position of body parts without needing to look at them.

Sense of Gravity – The labyrinth in the inner ear allows us to recognize our body's position relative to the ground.

Sense of Taste (Gustation) – More Than Four Basic Tastes – The newly discovered "umami" taste reveals that in addition to sweet, sour, bitter, and salty, we can also detect proteins.

Sense of Magnetism – Some studies suggest humans may have a sensitivity to magnetic fields, though it is not yet fully understood.

Sense of Vibration – The skin can detect subtle vibrations, helping us recognize vibrating objects or sounds transmitted through touch.

Sense of Fullness and Hunger – The brain and digestive system communicate to regulate appetite, signaling when we are hungry or full.

Sense of Pressure – Skin receptors respond to pressure, allowing us to feel touch and distinguish different textures.

Sense of Time – Although imprecise, we have an internal biological clock that gives us a sense of the passage of time.

Sense of Touch – A Complex Mechanism – Skin has different types of touch receptors that detect pressure, texture, vibrations, and movement.

Sense of Airflow – Receptors on the skin and around the nose detect subtle changes in airflow.

Sense of "Inner Hearing" – When we hum internally, the brain activates areas responsible for hearing, allowing us to "hear" imagined sounds.

Sense of Internal Warmth – Temperature receptors are also located inside the body, helping us sense things like fever.

Sense of Blood Pressure Changes – Baroreceptors in blood vessels monitor blood pressure and signal the brain when it changes.

Sense of Chewing and Swallowing – Receptors in the mouth control chewing force and allow for safe swallowing.

Sense of Auditory Spatial Perception – With two ears, we can accurately determine where sounds come from, aiding in spatial awareness.

Sense of Depth Perception – Having two eyes and the slight difference in each image helps us gauge distance and depth.

Sense of Physical Emotions – Certain emotions create physical sensations, like "butterflies in the stomach," as the body reacts to emotional states.

Section: Genetic Superpowers

People with Exceptional Bone Density – Individuals with a mutation in the LRP5 gene have extremely dense bones, making them nearly immune to fractures.

Natural Cold Resistance – Some people, like members of certain Inuit populations, carry genes that help them better endure extremely low temperatures.

Highly Developed Endurance – A mutation in the ACE gene, found in some athletes, allows for greater muscular endurance.

Pain Resistance – Some individuals have a mutation in the SCN9A gene, giving them a significantly higher pain tolerance.

People with "Good Cholesterol" – Mutations in the PCSK9 gene can reduce LDL ("bad") cholesterol levels and lower the risk of heart disease.

Ability to See Ultraviolet Light – Genetic changes, like those seen in individuals after certain lens surgeries, can enable UV spectrum vision.

Malaria Resistance – The mutation that causes sickle cell disease also provides protection against malaria, common in certain African regions.

Natural HIV Immunity – Some people have the CCR5-Δ32 mutation, which blocks HIV from infecting their cells.

Fast Recovery from Injuries – Variations in the MTHFR and ACTN3 genes are linked to quicker recovery after injuries.

Stronger Skin and Hair – Mutations in keratin-related genes make skin and hair more resilient to damage.

Exceptionally Low Lactic Acid Levels – Mutations in the PPARA gene allow muscles to use energy more efficiently, reducing fatigue.

Potential for Longevity – Certain genetic mutations related to insulin and lipid metabolism are associated with longer lifespans.

Rare Insensitivity to Cold – People with a TRPM8 gene mutation may have minimal sensitivity to cold temperatures.

Genetic Protection Against Alcoholism – A mutation in the ALDH2 gene causes alcohol intolerance, which reduces the risk of addiction.

Exceptional Muscle Strength – Mutations in the MSTN gene, which regulates muscle growth, can lead to unusually strong muscles.

Natural Protection Against Heart Disease – Unique variants in the APOA1 gene protect some individuals from atherosclerosis.

"Super Hearing" – Mutations in genes coding for proteins in the inner ear may allow individuals to hear frequencies outside the normal range.

Resistance to Obesity – Variations in the FTO gene influence fat metabolism, making it easier to maintain a healthy weight.

Enhanced Antioxidant Activity – Mutated genes like SOD2 can boost antioxidant enzyme production, slowing the aging process.

Exceptional Vision – A mutation in the LRP6 gene can improve visual abilities, including resolution and sharpness of sight.

Section: Unusual Human Behaviors

Hiccups That Last for Years – Some people experience chronic hiccups, lasting even decades, like Charles Osborne, who had hiccups for 68 years.

Spontaneous Laughter During Stress – Some people laugh in response to stress as a defense mechanism to ease tension.

Crying from Happiness – People may cry in response to intense joy, a behavior unique to humans.

Alien Hand Syndrome – A neurological disorder where one hand acts as if it has its own will, often making unintended movements.

Sleep Apnea – Some people stop breathing momentarily during sleep, leading to frequent awakenings and health impacts.

Eating While Asleep – Some individuals have sleep disorders that cause them to eat unconsciously at night, often with no memory of it in the morning.

Daydreaming – Some people experience brief, dream-like moments even while performing daily tasks.

"Contagious" Yawning – Yawning can be contagious, with some people yawning just from seeing or hearing others yawn.

Sneezing in Response to Bright Light – About 18-35% of people have a photic sneeze reflex, sneezing in reaction to intense light, especially sunlight.

Intense Blushing – For some, emotions like embarrassment trigger immediate and visible reddening of the skin.

Goosebumps from Emotions – Strong emotions, like listening to powerful music, can cause goosebumps.

Déjà Vu – The Feeling Something Has Happened Before – This common phenomenon gives people a sense that a current situation has occurred previously.

Synesthesia – Some people experience synesthesia, where they can "see" sounds or "hear" colors.

Hearing Their Own Thoughts as Voices – Though thoughts are usually silent, some people hear them as clear, audible voices.

Ability to "Control" Dreams – Lucid dreaming allows some individuals to direct their dreams consciously.

Intuitive Sense of Others' Moods – Empaths can feel other people's emotions, often without words or obvious cues.

"Hypnotic States" During Intense Focus – Some people enter a trance-like state when deeply focused on certain tasks.

"Butterflies in the Stomach" Due to Stress or Love – This is a physical reaction triggered by nerves before significant events or in the presence of a loved one.

Talking Aloud During Sleep – Some people talk while asleep, often triggered by strong emotions or stress.

Automatic Writing – In deep concentration, some people claim they can write texts that "come to them" without conscious control.

Chapter 3: Space and Astronomy

Section: Planets and Stars

Venus Rotates Opposite to Most Planets – Unlike Earth, Venus rotates backward, meaning the Sun rises in the west and sets in the east.

Mars Has the Tallest Mountain in the Solar System – Olympus Mons, a volcano about 22 kilometers high, is three times taller than Mount Everest.

Saturn is Lighter Than Water – If there were a large enough body of water, Saturn would float on its surface.

Jupiter Has the Most Moons of Any Planet – Jupiter has over 80 known moons, the largest being Ganymede, which is bigger than Mercury.

Stars "Twinkle" Because of Earth's Atmosphere – The twinkling effect is caused by atmospheric disturbances that alter the path of starlight.

The Sun Makes Up Over 99% of the Solar System's Mass – Its immense mass keeps planets, moons, and comets in its gravitational pull.

Uranus Rotates on Its Side – With an axial tilt of about 98 degrees, Uranus spins like a "rolling ball."

Water Exists on the Moon and Mars – Ice has been discovered on both, enhancing prospects for future human missions.

Pluto Has a Thinner Atmosphere than a Feather – Formerly classified as the ninth planet, Pluto has a thin, seasonal atmosphere primarily composed of nitrogen and methane.

The Sun is a White Star, Not Yellow – Though it appears yellow from Earth, the Sun emits full-spectrum light, giving it a white color.

Planet HD 189733b Rains Glass – With winds reaching 4,500 mph (7,000 km/h), glass particles "rain" through its atmosphere.

Neutron Stars Have Extreme Density – A teaspoon of matter from a neutron star would weigh about a billion tons on Earth.

Mercury is Closest to the Sun, But Not the Hottest – Venus, with its thick atmosphere, has higher temperatures despite being farther from the Sun.

Betelgeuse, a Red Giant, May Soon Explode as a Supernova – In its final life stage, Betelgeuse could go supernova within the next several thousand years.

Black Holes Can "Disappear" – Theoretically, black holes lose mass through Hawking radiation and could eventually evaporate entirely.

Some Stars We See Have Already Died – Light from stars travels thousands or even millions of years to reach us, so some may have already burned out.

Jupiter Protects Earth from Comets and Asteroids – Due to its massive gravitational field, Jupiter pulls or deflects many objects that could collide with Earth.

Pulsars Emit Regular Radio Pulses – These rapidly spinning neutron stars emit beams of radiation, acting like natural "lighthouses."

Venus is Hot Enough to Melt Lead – Surface temperatures reach around 470°C (878°F), enough to melt many metals.

The Sun Will Engulf Earth in About 5 Billion Years – Eventually, the Sun will expand into a red giant, potentially reaching Earth's orbit.

Section: Black Holes and Their Mysteries

Black Holes Form from Collapsed Stars – When a massive star reaches the end of its life, it collapses under its own gravity, creating a black hole.

The Event Horizon is the Point of No Return – Once an object crosses a black hole's event horizon, it cannot escape, not even light.

Black Holes Can "Grow" – As they consume matter, their mass and size increase, and their event horizon expands.

There Are Different Types of Black Holes – Black holes can be categorized as stellar or supermassive, with supermassive black holes found at galactic centers.

Supermassive Black Holes Weigh Millions of Suns – An example is Sagittarius A* at the center of the Milky Way, with a mass around 4 million times that of the Sun.

Black Holes Can "Create" New Stars – Accretion disks form around black holes, and the matter ejected in jets can trigger star formation.

Black Hole Jets Can Stretch Thousands of Light-Years – Some black holes emit jets of matter at incredible speeds, visible over vast distances.

Stephen Hawking Predicted Black Holes Can Evaporate – Known as Hawking radiation, this process suggests black holes could eventually dissipate.

Some Black Holes Can Travel Through Galaxies – "Wandering" black holes move through interstellar space.

Colliding Black Holes Generate Gravitational Waves – When two black holes collide, they produce gravitational waves, first detected in 2015.

Black Holes Cause Spacetime Effects – The space around a black hole is so curved that time moves more slowly near its event horizon.

Black Holes Can Act as Gravitational Lenses – Their gravity bends light, allowing us to see objects behind them.

Ingested Matter is Torn Apart at the Atomic Level – Known as spaghettification, intense gravity stretches matter into thin "threads" before it is consumed.

Black Holes Can Emit X-rays – As matter falls into a black hole, friction and gravity produce X-rays, which we can observe.

Some Theories Suggest Black Holes Lead to Other Universes – Hypothetical spacetime tunnels, or Einstein-Rosen bridges, are sometimes associated with black holes.

Not All Black Holes are Active – Black holes can be "dormant" if they lack access to matter to consume.

Black Holes Can Have "Photon Rings" – Photons can orbit a black hole on a stable path, creating a bright ring of light around the event horizon.

Gamma Radiation May Originate from Black Holes – Collisions of black holes or matter entering supermassive black holes can generate gamma-ray bursts.

Binary Black Hole Systems Create Complex Structures – In binary systems with a star, a black hole can draw matter from its companion, forming an accretion disk.

A Black Hole's Shadow Was Captured in 2019 – The first-ever image of a supermassive black hole's shadow, M87*, was captured by the Event Horizon Telescope, marking a historic achievement in astronomy.

Section: Light Phenomena

Auroras Are Created by Colliding Particles – Auroras (the aurora borealis in the north and aurora australis in the south) form when charged particles from the Sun collide with Earth's atmosphere.

Starlight Takes Thousands of Years to Reach Us – What we see in the night sky is the light from stars as it was hundreds or even millions of years ago.

The Blue Color of the Sky Is Due to Rayleigh Scattering – Shorter light waves (like blue) scatter more in the atmosphere than longer waves, making the sky appear blue.

Red Sun on the Horizon – During sunrise and sunset, light passes through a thicker layer of the atmosphere, scattering blue light and leaving reds visible.

Galactic Halo – Some galaxies have halos, a glowing light made of gas and stars surrounding the galactic core.

Rainbows Form from Light Refracting in Water Droplets – Light passes through raindrops, refracting and splitting into a colorful arc.

Rings Around the Moon – Called a lunar halo, these rings form when moonlight refracts through ice crystals in the atmosphere.

The "Green Flash" at Sunset – A brief green flash can sometimes be seen at sunset or sunrise, caused by light refraction.

Light from Supernovae Is Visible for Years – Supernova explosions emit vast amounts of light, visible long after the initial blast.

Moonlight is Reflected Sunlight – The Moon doesn't produce its own light; we see it because of sunlight reflected off its surface.

Meteorology Creates "Sundogs" – These are bright spots on either side of the Sun, caused by light refracting through ice crystals.

Laser Light Can Be Visible from Space – Lasers emit light in coherent waves, allowing it to travel significant distances without scattering.

The Milky Way Appears as a Bright Streak in the Sky – This is the combined light of billions of stars in the disk of our galaxy.

Comets Leave Light Trails – As comets approach the Sun, they release gas and dust, forming a visible tail.

A Full Moon Affects Star Observing – The brightness of the full moon makes it harder to see faint objects in the night sky.

Light from Distant Galaxies Appears Red Due to Redshift – This effect is caused by the expanding universe, which shifts galaxies' light toward the red end of the spectrum.

Burning Meteors – Meteor Showers – When meteoroids enter Earth's atmosphere, they burn up, creating bright trails in the sky.

Mirrored Reflections on Water Create Optical Effects – Reflected light refracts on rippling water, creating a shimmering and waving effect.

Fireballs – Exceptionally bright meteors (bolides) often break into smaller fragments as they burn up.

Zodiacal Light – This faint light, visible at night, is caused by sunlight scattering on dust particles in the plane of the Solar System.

Section: Life Beyond Earth

Experiments on the International Space Station (ISS) Study Life's Potential in Space – Scientists test how microorganisms handle the extreme conditions of space.

Mars is a Primary Target for the Search for Life – Discoveries suggest that Mars once had rivers and oceans, increasing the likelihood of past life.

Europa, Jupiter's Moon, May Harbor an Ocean Beneath Its Ice – It's believed that liquid water under Europa's icy crust could provide conditions conducive to life.

Enceladus, Saturn's Moon, Ejects Water Geysers – Analysis of these geysers has detected organic compounds, which may support life.

Organic Particles Found on Comets – Comets like 67P/Churyumov-Gerasimenko contain organic particles that may be key to the origin of life.

Extremophiles on Earth Suggest Life's Resilience in Harsh Conditions – Organisms living in extreme environments, like hot springs or deep-sea vents, show that life can thrive in unusual conditions.

Microorganisms Can Survive in Space – Certain bacteria and viruses can withstand prolonged exposure to vacuum and radiation.

Phosphine in Venus's Atmosphere as a Potential Indicator of Life – The discovery of phosphine in Venus's clouds has led to speculation about unknown biological processes.

Titan, Saturn's Moon, Has Lakes of Liquid Methane – Although conditions are extreme, exotic life forms that use methane may be possible.

Possibility of "Warm" Planets in Other Stars' Habitable Zones – Planets in the "habitable zone" may have liquid water, which is essential for life.

Discovery of Earth-sized Exoplanets – Astronomers have identified several exoplanets with Earth-like conditions, raising the chances of life.

METI: Sending Messages to Potential Civilizations – METI (Messaging Extraterrestrial Intelligence) programs send signals in hopes of contacting other life forms.

Searching for Radio Signals from Space – Projects like SETI analyze radio signals for patterns that could come from intelligent civilizations.

Mars Missions Aim to Search for Traces of Life – Rovers like Perseverance are equipped with tools for geological and chemical analysis on Mars.

Amino Acids, the Building Blocks of Proteins, Found on Meteorites – These discoveries suggest that life's building blocks may be present in space.

Subsurface Oceans on Jupiter and Saturn's Moons – Oceans hidden beneath icy surfaces may be warmed by geothermal activity, potentially supporting life.

Panspermia Hypothesis – This theory suggests that life may have originated in space and been transported to Earth by meteorites.

Astrobiology Studies the Potential for Life on Exoplanets – This field analyzes conditions on other planets to determine their potential for supporting life.

Potential Microbiology in Planetary Atmospheres – Some theories suggest that upper layers of atmospheres on certain planets may contain microbial life.

The Human Genome Contains Viral Genes – This evidence suggests that life on Earth may have been influenced by external factors, supporting the panspermia hypothesis.

Section: Planetary Motions and Mysterious Phenomena

Planetary Retrograde Motion – This phenomenon, where planets like Mars appear to move backward in the sky, is an effect of Earth's motion relative to other planets.

Earth's Axial Precession – The tilt of Earth's axis changes slowly over thousands of years, causing the position of the North Star to shift over time.

Mercury's Mysterious Orbital Deviation – Mercury's orbit is influenced by the Sun's gravity, with small deviations explained by Einstein's theory of relativity.

Planetary Migration in the Early Solar System – Jupiter and Saturn are believed to have moved closer to and farther from the Sun, affecting the Solar System's formation.

Earth's Pole Shifts – Earth's magnetic field shifts over thousands of years, altering the poles and impacting navigation and life.

The Mysterious Object 'Oumuamua – Discovered in 2017, this interstellar object entered the Solar System and moved in a puzzling manner.

Spaghettification Near a Black Hole – The intense gravity of black holes stretches objects along their axis, creating "threads" of matter.

Chaotic Asteroid Orbits – Some asteroids have orbits that change unpredictably due to gravitational interactions with planets.

The Yarkovsky Effect – Heat emitted from a rotating asteroid's surface can alter its orbit over time.

Uranus's Tilted Axis – Uranus rotates at nearly a 98-degree angle, causing its poles to point toward the Sun.

Mars's Atmosphere Loss – Mars has lost most of its atmosphere, possibly stripped away by solar wind, which remains a mystery.

Dark Rings of Saturn – Parts of Saturn's rings are darker and denser, indicating differences in material composition.

Retrograde Moons of Jupiter and Saturn – Some moons orbit in the opposite direction of their planet's rotation, suggesting they may be captured objects.

Jupiter's Rapid Rotation – Jupiter rotates faster than any other planet, completing a full rotation in just under 10 hours.

Extreme Temperature Fluctuations on Mercury – With no atmosphere, Mercury experiences extreme temperature differences between day and night, from -173°C to 427°C.

The Moon's Gravity Affects Earth – The tides on Earth result from the gravitational pull of the Moon.

Hypothetical Planet Nine – Evidence suggests a large, undiscovered planet at the edge of the Solar System influencing the movement of distant objects.

Extreme Elliptical Orbits of Comets – Comets follow highly elliptical orbits, returning to the Sun after hundreds or even thousands of years.

Gravitational Microlensing – Massive objects in space can bend light, allowing us to observe distant stars that would otherwise be invisible.

Venus's Anomalous Rotation – Venus rotates very slowly and in the opposite direction of most planets, a mystery that scientists are still investigating.

Chapter 4: Plants and Ecology

Section: Carnivorous Plants that Feed on Animals

Venus Flytrap (Dionaea muscipula) – Known for its rapid-closing leaf traps that snap shut when an insect touches special trigger hairs.

Sundew (Drosera) – This plant's leaves are covered with sticky droplets that attract insects, which then get trapped and digested by enzymes.

Pitcher Plant (Nepenthes) – With pitcher-shaped leaves containing digestive liquid, insects fall inside and are digested.

Butterwort (Pinguicula) – The sticky leaves trap small insects, which are then digested with the help of enzymes.

Waterwheel Plant (Aldrovanda vesiculosa) – An aquatic plant with traps that snap around small aquatic organisms.

Forked Sundew (Drosera binata) – Its forked leaves are covered with sticky hairs that ensnare insects.

Pitcher Plant (Sarracenia) – This plant has pitcher-shaped leaves that trap and digest prey inside.

Sun Pitcher (Heliamphora) – A mountain pitcher plant with leaves that form traps to attract and digest insects.

Corkscrew Plant (Genlisea) – An aquatic plant with roots that act as traps for small aquatic organisms.

Bladderwort (Utricularia) – An aquatic plant that captures tiny organisms in vacuum-powered bladder traps.

Rainbow Plant (Byblis) – Named for its sticky leaves that attract and digest insects.

Trigger Plant (Stylidium) – Produces flowers with mobile stamens that can trap insects, aiding in digestion.

Dewy Pine (Drosophyllum) – Has aromatic, sticky leaves that attract and digest insects.

Brocchinia reducta – A member of the pineapple family found in the Amazon, with traps that digest insects.

Roridula – Works symbiotically with predatory insects that feed on the trapped prey.

Devil's Claw (Ibicella lutea) – A South American plant with sticky leaves that capture insects, supporting predatory insects that feed on them.

Philcoxia – A Brazilian plant with underground leaves that trap and digest nematodes.

Brocchinia hechtioides – Similar to Brocchinia reducta, with a pitcher trap containing digestive enzymes for catching insects.

Roridula dentata – Produces sticky hairs to trap insects, which are then consumed by predatory insects that live symbiotically with it.

King Sundew (Dionaea regia) – Related to the Venus flytrap, using mechanical traps to capture insects.

Section: Plant Defense Mechanisms

Cactus Spines – Spines protect cacti from herbivores that would otherwise access the water stored in their fleshy stems.

Toxic Alkaloids in Deadly Nightshade – Deadly nightshade contains toxic compounds like atropine, which deter animals and insects.

Milky Sap in Fig Trees – Fig trees release a sticky, often poisonous sap that discourages insects and mammals.

Formic Acid in Nettles – The fine hairs on nettle leaves release formic acid, causing a painful stinging sensation on contact.

Chemical Compounds in Oak Trees – Oak leaves produce tannins, which are toxic or unpalatable to many herbivores.

Poisonous Glycosides in Cassava – Raw cassava contains cyanogenic glycosides, which convert to cyanide and are toxic.

Essential Oils in Lavender – Lavender produces essential oils that repel insects.

Sticky Mucilage in Sticky Wattle – This sticky substance deters insects and makes climbing difficult.

Bitter Taste in Wormwood – Wormwood produces bitter compounds that effectively repel animals.

Odor Emission in Skunk Cabbage – This plant releases an unpleasant odor that repels animals and insects.

Hallucinogenic Compounds in Jimson Weed – This plant produces psychoactive substances that deter herbivores.

Leaf-Closing Mechanism in Mimosa – Mimosa leaves fold up when touched, discouraging herbivores from further attempts to eat it.

Toxic Sap in Spurges – Many plants in the spurge family contain sap that is toxic and irritating to the skin.

Hawthorn Thorns – Thorns on hawthorn trees deter animals from eating their fruit and leaves.

Bitter Substances in Apple Trees – Apple tree leaves produce compounds that deter insects from chewing on them.

Defensive Thorns on Acacia – Some acacia species produce thorns and provide shelter for ants that defend the plant from herbivores.

Harmful Compounds in Lily of the Valley – The entire plant contains glycosides that are toxic to humans and animals.

Bitterness in Burdock – The roots and leaves of burdock have a bitter taste that deters potential grazers.

Stinging Hairs in Stinging Burdock – The hairs contain irritating compounds that cause a burning sensation on contact.

Sulfurous Oils in Mustard Plants – Mustard produces pungent sulfurous oils that repel insects and some herbivores.

Section: Extreme Habitats

Hydrothermal Vent Plants in Deep Oceans – Plants around hydrothermal vents on the ocean floor withstand extreme pressure and high temperatures.

Arctic and Antarctic Mosses – These plants survive freezing conditions and long periods of darkness.

Desert Plants like Cacti – Adapted to extreme drought, cacti store water in their stems and have spines instead of leaves.

High-Altitude Succulents in the Andes – Plants like Puya raimondii are adapted to extreme cold and low oxygen levels.

Salt-Tolerant Plants (Halophytes) – Found in salty environments like salt marshes, they can expel excess salt from their cells.

Heavy Metal-Tolerant Plants – Some species, known as metallophytes, grow on soils contaminated with heavy metals such as lead and zinc.

Tropical Epiphytes like Bromeliads – Growing on other plants in humid rainforests, they absorb water directly from the air.

Tundra Shrubs like Dwarf Birch – Adapted to survive in permafrost regions of the tundra.

Volcanic Soil Plants like Nolina – Can grow on lava rocks and survive high temperatures and low moisture.

Water Plants in Acidic Lakes – Some aquatic plants thrive in lakes with very low pH, tolerating high acidity.

Mangroves on Tropical Coasts – These trees grow in salty seawater and have a root system adapted to low oxygen levels and soft soil stabilization.

Marsh Plants like Bulrushes – Adapted to low-oxygen water, often with root systems that contain air spaces.

Desert Sand Dune Plants like Ephemerals – Bloom and grow rapidly after rare rains, completing their life cycle before water evaporates.

Rainforest Trees with Shallow Roots – Tall trees in nutrient-poor, wet soils have wide, shallow root systems to stabilize in the moist ground.

Coastal Dune Plants – Adapted to salt and shifting sands, such as dune grasses and heathers.

High-Mountain Plants like Edelweiss – Have protective hairs that shield them from cold and intense UV radiation.

Flood-Adapted Plants like Water Lilies – With floating leaves and flowers, they thrive in submerged environments.

Lichens on Rocks – Survive on bare rocks, drawing moisture and nutrients directly from the air.

Taiga Region Plants – Trees like pines have needles that minimize water loss, helping them endure long, freezing winters.

Wind-Resistant Plants like Prairie Grasses – Deep-rooted grasses are stabilized against strong winds and soil erosion.

Section: The Role of Plants in Ecosystems

Oxygen Production – Through photosynthesis, plants produce oxygen, essential for the respiration of most organisms on Earth.

Carbon Dioxide Absorption – Plants absorb CO_2, helping to reduce atmospheric levels and combat global warming.

Soil Stabilization – Plant roots prevent soil erosion, helping to retain water and nutrients in the soil.

Providing Food – Plants are a primary food source for many herbivores and indirectly for predators.

Habitat Creation – Plants like trees and shrubs provide shelter and nesting sites for numerous animals.

Water Cycle Maintenance – Plant transpiration releases water into the atmosphere, influencing rainfall and sustaining the water cycle.

Providing Shelter – Trees and shrubs offer cover for small animals and birds, protecting them from predators and harsh weather.

Biodiversity Support – Plants support biological diversity by providing food and shelter for many species.

Medicinal Substance Production – Many plants provide compounds used in traditional and modern medicine.

Nutrient Accumulation – Plants accumulate nitrogen and other nutrients, releasing them into the soil for future plant generations.

Temperature Regulation – Forests and green areas act as natural air conditioners, cooling surrounding areas through transpiration.

Resources for Industry – Wood, fibers, and plant oils are essential for products ranging from furniture to textiles.

Soil and Water Purification – Plants like reeds filter pollutants, helping to clean soil and groundwater.

Combating Desertification – Plants prevent desert spread by stabilizing soil and retaining moisture.

Flood Prevention – Plant root systems in wetlands absorb water, reducing the risk of flooding.

Creating Microclimates – Large plant clusters create their own microclimates, influencing humidity and temperature nearby.

Symbiosis with Microorganisms – Plants live in symbiosis with bacteria and fungi, aiding nutrient absorption and disease protection.

Pollination Support – Plants attract pollinators that transfer pollen between flowers, enabling reproduction.

Energy Supply in the Food Web – As primary producers, plants are the foundation of the food web, providing energy to all consumer levels.

Shaping the Landscape – Plants help shape terrain, contributing to the formation of various ecosystems such as forests, meadows, and wetlands.

Section: Plants That Predict the Weather

Oxalis (Wood Sorrel) – The leaves of this plant fold or close before rain, indicating incoming moisture.

White Clover – Before rain, the leaves of white clover fold or press close to the ground to protect against moisture.

Evening Primrose – The flowers of evening primrose close before a storm or rain as a protective response.

Field Horsetail – Before rain, horsetail shifts its branches to a more upright position.

Dandelion – Dandelion flowers close as rain approaches to protect the seeds from moisture.

Marigold – Marigold flowers close before rain, providing natural protection from wet weather.

Field Bindweed – The leaves and flowers of this plant close before rain, protecting the interior from excess water.

Water Lily – Water lilies close their flowers before rain, and their opening often signals sunny weather.

Corn – Corn tassels curl up before rain to protect its pollen from being washed away.

Common Nettle – Nettle leaves stiffen and slightly rise before rain, helping the plant withstand heavy downpours.

Elecampane **– Its flowers close when atmospheric pressure drops,** often indicating upcoming rain.

Lobelia – Lobelia flowers close before rain to protect their delicate petals.

Daisy – Daisy flowers close at night and in rainy weather, protecting the inner parts of the plant.

Primrose – Before rain, primrose leaves adjust to lie closer to the ground.

Common Plantain – Plantain leaves change position and may become stiffer before rainfall.

Fern – Some fern species curl their leaves before rain to prevent damage.

European Larch – The needles of the European larch become denser and press closer to branches before rainfall.

Sage – Sage leaves may become fleshier and stiffer before rain, helping them handle moisture.

Violet – Violet flowers close before rain, and their opening often signals improving weather.

Peony – Peony flowers close before rainfall to protect their interior from getting wet.

Chapter 5: Culture and History

Section: Strange Historical Customs

Mummification of Cats in Ancient Egypt – Egyptians mummified cats as offerings to the goddess Bastet, believing they would bring good fortune in the afterlife.

Blood Baths as a Health Remedy in Ancient Greece – It was believed that bathing in animal blood had healing properties and could improve health.

Facial Scarification as a Beauty Symbol in African Cultures – Ritual facial scars were symbols of tribal affiliation and beauty in some African cultures.

Beak Masks Worn by Plague Doctors During the Black Death – Doctors wore beak-like masks filled with herbs, thinking this would protect them from the "miasma" or bad air causing the plague.

Foot Binding in Ancient China – For centuries, Chinese girls' feet were bound as a symbol of beauty and high social status.

Cranial Shaping of Newborns in Andean Cultures – Some South American cultures shaped infants' skulls to indicate elite status.

Fasting Rituals in Medieval Monasteries – Certain monastic orders practiced fasting, believing that hunger purified the soul and strengthened the spirit.

Bloodletting as a Medieval Treatment – Bloodletting was a common medical practice, thought to remove "bad blood" and cure illness.

Tongue Tattooing Rituals of the Maori – Maori tattooed their tongues as a sign of courage and clan identity.

Self-Mutilation in Religious Rituals – In some Middle Eastern cultures, self-inflicted wounds were part of devotion to gods.

Death Embrace in Ancient Persia as a Form of Regicide – It was believed that dying in the embrace of a loved one would allow the soul to pass peacefully to the afterlife.

Egyptian Mothers Using Opium to Soothe Children – Egyptian mothers would give small doses of opium to children to help them sleep.

Fortune Telling with Animal Entrails in Ancient Rome – Romans practiced haruspicy, interpreting animal entrails to predict the future.

Human Sacrifices in Aztec Culture – The Aztecs sacrificed humans, believing their blood sustained the gods and preserved the world.

Finger Amputation as a Mourning Ritual in New Guinea – Some tribes amputated fingers as a sign of grief after the death of a loved one.

Neck Rings Worn by Padaung Women – Women of the Padaung tribe wore metal rings around their necks to elongate them, a symbol of beauty.

Self-Mummification Practice in Japan – Buddhist monks practiced Sokushinbutsu, self-mummification, as a path to holiness.

Consumption of Ancestors' Remains by Amazon Tribes – Certain Amazonian tribes consumed the ashes of their ancestors, believing it kept their spirits close.

Viking Tradition of "Catching the Wind" in Bags – Vikings believed they could "catch the wind" in a bag to ensure a successful sea journey.

Tibetan Sky Burials – In Tibetan culture, bodies of the deceased were left on mountain tops to be consumed by birds, symbolizing the cycle of life.

Section: Phenomena of Human Communities

Swarm Mentality in Large Gatherings – Similar to social insects, some human communities display "swarm" behavior, making decisions collectively during large gatherings.

Rites of Passage into Adulthood – Different cultures have initiation ceremonies for adulthood, such as the Jewish Bar Mitzvah or the Native American Vision Quest.

Tribal Communities with Strong Collective Bonds – In tribes like the African Maasai, a strong sense of community leads to shared resources and child-rearing responsibilities.

Taboos as Social Regulation – Many societies use taboos to control behaviors that could disrupt social norms, such as dietary restrictions in Islam and Judaism.

Gift Culture on the Trobriand Islands – In Trobriand societies, gift exchange is highly valued, strengthening social bonds and hierarchies.

The Caste System in India – The Indian caste system is a long-standing social hierarchy affecting social life and marriage.

Samurai Hierarchy in Japan – The samurai formed an elite class with a rigid hierarchy that shaped Japanese society for centuries.

Rural-to-Urban Migration – The movement from rural areas to cities for better opportunities has been ongoing for centuries.

Clan Loyalty in African and Scottish Societies – Clan-based social structures, like those among Scottish Highlanders, are built on loyalty to the family group.

Kibbutz in Israel as an Egalitarian Community – Kibbutzim operate as egalitarian communities where resources are shared, and everyone works for the collective.

Pyramidal Societies in Ancient Egypt – Ancient Egypt had a highly stratified society with the pharaoh at the top, revered as a deity.

Cultural Blending and Globalization – Cultures around the world adopt elements from others, creating new values and lifestyles, such as the spread of Western culture.

Matrilineal Societies like the Minangkabau – The Minangkabau of Indonesia pass land and inheritance through the mother's line, strengthening women's roles in society.

Self-Organization During Disasters – Communities often self-organize in times of crisis, like earthquakes or floods, as locals coordinate relief efforts.

Hermitic Communities like the Amish – The Amish maintain traditional ways of life, avoiding modern technology and adhering to communal principles.

"Share the Wealth" in Maori Culture – The Maori principle of manaakitanga obliges communities to care for each other and share resources.

"Monastic Communities" – Monasteries and convents function as isolated communities focused on religious beliefs and a shared lifestyle.

Hunter-Gatherer Societies and Nomadism – Hunter-gatherer groups, like the San Bushmen, move to find food and maintain ecological balance.

Festivals and Community Rituals – In cultures like Japan and South America, regular festivals reinforce a sense of community and belonging.

Tribal Negotiations as Conflict Resolution – In traditional societies, such as some African tribes, conflicts are resolved through negotiation and elder mediation.

Section: Mysterious Figures and Their Stories

Nostradamus – A 16th-century French astrologer and prophet known for his predictions, which continue to intrigue and spark controversy.

Rasputin – A Russian mystic and advisor to the Romanov family, alleged to have wielded immense influence over Tsar Nicholas II's court, ultimately murdered under mysterious circumstances.

King Arthur – A legendary British ruler who, according to myth, reigned from Camelot and was associated with Merlin the wizard and the quest for the Holy Grail.

Cleopatra – The last queen of Egypt from the Ptolemaic dynasty, renowned for her charisma and relationships with Julius Caesar and Mark Antony.

The Man in the Iron Mask – A mysterious prisoner in France whose identity remains unknown, inspiring countless theories.

Vlad the Impaler (Dracula) – A 15th-century ruler of Wallachia, infamous for his cruelty, who inspired the fictional character Dracula.

Saint Joan of Arc – A French national hero who claimed divine visions and led an army against the English in the Hundred Years' War.

Greta Garbo – The enigmatic Hollywood actress who withdrew from public life at the peak of her fame, leaving her personal life shrouded in mystery.

The Templars – A medieval knightly order that met an abrupt end, with their wealth and treasures allegedly lost, fueling legends and conspiracy theories.

Kaspar Hauser – A mysterious young man who appeared in 19th-century Germany, claiming he had been held captive in isolation his entire life.

Robin Hood – The legendary English outlaw said to have stolen from the rich to give to the poor, though his existence remains unconfirmed.

Elizabeth Báthory – A Hungarian countess accused of murdering young girls and bathing in their blood to maintain youth; her story remains contentious.

Grigori Rasputin – Known for his enigmatic charisma and alleged healing powers, Rasputin became a symbol of the fall of the Russian Empire.

Ludwig II of Bavaria – Known as the "Fairy Tale King" for his elaborate castles, he died under mysterious circumstances.

D.B. Cooper – A man who hijacked a plane in 1971 and parachuted away with a large sum of money, never to be found.

Jack the Ripper – A mysterious 19th-century London serial killer who murdered five women; his identity remains unknown.

Nikola Tesla – An inventor and visionary whose advanced ideas continue to inspire controversy and conspiracy theories.

Mary Celeste – A ship found adrift in the Atlantic with no crew aboard, leading to many theories about its mysterious fate.

The Mothman of Point Pleasant – An alleged figure with red eyes seen near Point Pleasant in the USA, believed to be linked to tragic events.

Dorothy Eady (Omm Sety) – A British woman who claimed to be the reincarnation of an ancient Egyptian priestess, fascinating archaeologists with her knowledge of Egypt.

Section: Ancient Beliefs and Facts

Geocentrism in Ancient Greece – The Greeks believed Earth was the center of the universe, with all other celestial bodies revolving around it.

Pyramids as Stairways to Heaven – Ancient Egyptians saw pyramids as symbols of the pharaoh's ascension to eternal life and as a pathway to the gods.

The Four Elements of the World – Ancient Greeks, like Aristotle, believed that everything was composed of four elements: earth, water, fire, and air.

Belief in a Flat Earth – Many ancient cultures, including the Babylonians, thought the Earth was flat and rested on foundations.

Divine Origin of Illnesses – In numerous cultures, diseases were seen as punishment from gods or actions of evil spirits, and treatments often involved rituals.

Egyptian Belief in the Afterlife – Egyptians believed that after death, the soul would undergo judgment by Osiris; if deemed pure, it would enter the Land of the Dead.

St. Elmo's Fire as a Divine Sign – Ancient sailors believed that the glow on masts during storms was a message from the gods.

Astrology as a Tool for Predicting the Future – In Babylon and later Rome, astrology was used to predict events and influence political decisions.

The Myth of Atlantis as a Lost Paradise – Ancient Greeks, particularly Plato, described Atlantis as an advanced civilization that was lost to divine retribution.

Sacred Trees as Homes for Spirits – In cultures such as the Celts, trees were seen as sacred, inhabited by spirits and magical beings.

Vampires in Ancient Mesopotamia – Mesopotamian beliefs included creatures that would return from the afterlife to feed on the blood of the living.

Soul Migration and Reincarnation – In India, belief in reincarnation and karma has existed for centuries, where souls are reborn in new bodies according to their actions.

Belief in the Magical Properties of Metals – Ancient Greeks thought silver had healing qualities, while gold was associated with strength and divine powers.

The Epic of Gilgamesh as a Reflection of Sumerian Beliefs – This epic deals with themes of life, death, and immortality. reflecting the Sumerians' view of power and divinity in rulers.

Belief in the Divine Origin of Rulers – In ancient Egypt, the pharaoh was considered the embodiment of the god Horus, bridging gods and humans.

Belief in Mythical Creatures like Griffins and Unicorns – People believed in mythical animals with supernatural powers, often as protectors of treasures or with magical abilities.

Delphi as the Center of the Universe – Ancient Greeks viewed the oracle at Delphi as a place to seek guidance directly from the gods.

Chinese Concept of Yin and Yang – The Chinese believed that the universe was balanced by two opposing forces: Yin and Yang.

Kalokagathia – The Ideal of Beauty and Goodness – The Greeks held that one should strive to combine physical beauty with moral virtue.

Reverence for Sacred Animals – In various cultures, like ancient Egypt and India, certain animals such as cows and cats were considered sacred and worshipped.

Section: Innovations That Changed the World

The Wheel – Invented around 3500 BCE in Mesopotamia, the wheel revolutionized transportation and technological development across many aspects of life.

Printing Press – Johannes Gutenberg's invention of the movable-type printing press in the 15th century enabled mass dissemination of knowledge, fueling education and the Renaissance.

Electricity – Discoveries related to electricity and Thomas Edison's invention of the light bulb in the 19th century transformed daily life, enabling work and activity at night.

Computer – Early computers like ENIAC allowed calculations on an unprecedented scale, initiating the development of information technology.

Internet – Created in the 1960s and popularized in the 1990s, the Internet enabled global communication and access to information in an unprecedented way.

Steam Engine – In the 18th century, James Watt's improvements to the steam engine spurred the Industrial Revolution and the development of transportation, especially railroads.

Penicillin – Alexander Fleming's discovery of penicillin in 1928 revolutionized medicine, saving millions by effectively treating bacterial infections.

Automobile – Henry Ford's assembly line in the early 20th century made mass car production possible, revolutionizing personal and industrial transportation.

Vaccination – Edward Jenner's first vaccine in 1796 contributed to the elimination of diseases such as smallpox.

Telephone – Alexander Graham Bell's invention of the telephone in 1876 enabled instant long-distance communication.

Kerosene Lamp – Ignacy Łukasiewicz's kerosene lamp in the 19th century provided nighttime lighting before widespread electricity.

Airplane – The Wright brothers' first flight in 1903 paved the way for passenger aviation and air transport.

Laser – Theodore Maiman's invention of the laser in 1960 laid the foundation for optical technologies used in medicine, telecommunications, and industry.

GPS (Global Positioning System) – Introduced widely in the 1990s, GPS allows precise location tracking, revolutionizing transport and tourism.

Barcode – Norman Joseph Woodland's invention of the barcode in 1949 enabled automation in sales and inventory management.

Microprocessor – Intel's 1971 invention of the microprocessor transformed electronics and enabled the development of personal computers.

Nuclear Power Plants – Nuclear technology, developed in the 1950s, provided the means to generate vast amounts of electricity.

3D Printer – 3D printing technology enabled on-demand production of prototypes and parts, transforming industries from medicine to architecture.

Hormonal Contraception – The introduction of the birth control pill in the 1960s gave women more control over family planning.

Communication Satellites – The development of satellites enabled global telecommunications, TV broadcasts, and worldwide information access.

Chapter 6: Technology and Inventions

Section: Accidental Inventions

Penicillin – Alexander Fleming discovered the first antibiotic, penicillin, when he noticed that mold killed bacteria on a culture dish.

Microwave Oven – Percy Spencer invented the microwave after noticing that a chocolate bar in his pocket melted from microwave exposure during his work with magnetrons.

Post-it Notes Adhesive – Spencer Silver developed a weak adhesive initially thought useless, but it later found a purpose in sticky notes.

Stainless Steel – Harry Brearley discovered stainless steel while experimenting with metal alloys to create corrosion-resistant gun barrels.

Potato Chips – Chef George Crum accidentally created potato chips by slicing potatoes very thinly and frying them in response to a customer complaint.

Saccharin (Artificial Sweetener) – Chemist Constantin Fahlberg invented saccharin after tasting a sweet substance on his hands that he forgot to wash after work.

Plastic (Bakelite) – Leo Baekeland, in search of a synthetic alternative to shellac, invented Bakelite, the first synthetic plastic, which transformed industries.

Velcro – George de Mestral noticed how burrs clung to his clothes, inspiring him to invent the hook-and-loop fastening system known as Velcro.

Chewing Gum – The discovery that mixing resin with other ingredients created a chewable, elastic substance led to the invention of chewing gum.

Matches – John Walker accidentally created matches by mixing chemicals that ignited when rubbed against a surface.

X-rays – Wilhelm Röntgen discovered X-rays when he noticed a mysterious glow on a phosphorescent screen during radiation experiments.

Rubber Vulcanization – Charles Goodyear accidentally discovered vulcanization when a rubber and sulfur mixture fell onto a hot stove, making rubber more durable.

Teflon – Roy Plunkett discovered Teflon while researching refrigerant gases when his sample unexpectedly turned into a smooth, non-stick material.

Dynamite – Alfred Nobel invented dynamite by stabilizing nitroglycerin with diatomaceous earth during his experiments with explosives.

Viagra – Originally tested for hypertension and angina, Viagra's effects in other areas were discovered during clinical trials.

Play-Doh – Initially created as a wallpaper cleaner, Play-Doh became popular as a children's toy.

Safety Glass – Chemist Edouard Benedictus accidentally invented safety glass when a glass vial coated with cellulose didn't shatter completely after being dropped.

Super Glue (Cyanoacrylate) – Cyanoacrylate was discovered accidentally during experiments with sighting materials; it turned out to be a very strong adhesive.

Insulin – Insulin as a treatment for diabetes was discovered by Frederick Banting and Charles Best while experimenting with dog pancreases.

Pacemaker – Wilson Greatbatch accidentally invented the pacemaker when he used an incorrect resistor in an experimental device, leading to its medical application.

Section: Unusual Uses of Everyday Items

Aluminum Foil to Sharpen Scissors – Folding a piece of foil and cutting through it with scissors can help keep the blades sharper.

Banana Peel for Polishing Shoes – The inside of a banana peel can work as a natural polish for leather shoes.

Chalk to Absorb Moisture in Closets – Placing chalk in closets or boxes absorbs moisture and helps prevent mold.

Eraser for Cleaning Keyboard – A soft eraser can remove grime and smudges from a computer keyboard's surface.

Soaking Clothes in Vinegar Before Washing – Vinegar helps prevent colors from fading and neutralizes unpleasant odors.

Soap Nuts as Natural Laundry Detergent – Soap nuts contain saponins that act as a natural laundry detergent.

Wax Crayons as Emergency Candles – In a pinch, a wax crayon can be lit and will burn for a few minutes.

Plastic Straws to Store Jewelry Chains – Threading chains through straws prevents them from tangling during travel.

Sponge to Dust Blinds – A damp sponge can effectively remove dust from blinds.

Tea Bags to Neutralize Odors in Shoes – Used tea bags can absorb odors when placed inside shoes.

Spoon for Peeling Ginger – Scraping ginger with a spoon removes the peel more precisely than a knife.

Ketchup for Cleaning Copper – The acid in ketchup works well for polishing copper items and removing tarnish.

Newspaper for Cleaning Windows – Using newspaper to clean windows leaves fewer streaks than paper towels.

Lemon Peel to Deodorize the Dishwasher – A lemon peel freshens up the dishwasher and eliminates residual odors.

Microwaving a Kitchen Sponge to Sanitize – Heating a damp sponge in the microwave for a few seconds kills bacteria.

Hair Dryer to Remove Wax Stains – Hot air from a hair dryer melts wax on fabric, making it easier to remove.

Toothpaste to Polish Silver – A small amount of toothpaste can restore shine to silver items.

Lint Roller for Dusting Lampshades – A lint roller effectively removes dust from fabric lampshades.

Clear Nail Polish as a Sealant for Small Scratches – Clear nail polish can seal small scratches on surfaces like phone screens.

Petroleum Jelly to Prevent Rust – Applying petroleum jelly to metal items, especially garden tools, prevents rust formation.

Section: Technologies That Surpass Our Understanding

Artificial Intelligence and Deep Learning – AI can recognize patterns and make decisions that are not always fully understood by its creators, especially within complex neural networks.

Quantum Mechanics and Quantum Computers – Quantum computers operate based on principles like superposition and entanglement, which remain deeply mysterious to scientists.

Quantum Cryptography – The use of quantum entanglement for secure data transmission is virtually unbreakable, yet the mechanism is challenging to fully comprehend.

Machine Learning Algorithms – These algorithms build models based on data to predict future events, yet even their creators may not fully understand every decision.

Antimatter – While we can create antimatter in labs, its exact nature and purpose in the cosmos are still unclear.

Nuclear Fusion – Fusion theoretically offers clean energy, but controlling and sustaining stable fusion reactions at scale is not yet achievable.

Genomics and Gene Editing – Technologies like CRISPR allow gene editing, though the full implications and understanding of genetic interactions remain beyond our reach.

Tissue Engineering – Creating organs and tissues in laboratories is possible, but fully replicating biological functions across an entire organism is complex and largely uncharted.

Brain-Computer Interface (BCI) – BCIs enable communication with devices through thought, yet are limited by the unresolved mysteries surrounding consciousness.

Autonomous Drones – Fully autonomous drones can operate independently, but their responses to novel situations aren't always predictable.

Metamaterials – These materials can manipulate light and sound waves in ways that challenge current understanding of their full implications.

Graphene and Two-Dimensional Materials – Graphene has remarkable conductive and structural properties, yet its applications and safety implications are still under study.

Cryptocurrencies and Blockchain – Despite their popularity, the long-term economic and environmental impacts of cryptocurrencies and blockchain technology remain uncertain.

Holograms and 3D Imaging Technology – Realistic holograms are feasible, but the broader applications, including potential in education or psychology, are not yet fully understood.

Synthetic Biology and Artificial Life – Creating artificial life in the lab raises ethical and technological questions, with unpredictable consequences.

Universe Simulation Models – Simulations that model the universe's evolution attempt to replicate cosmic principles, yet our grasp of fundamental cosmic laws remains incomplete.

Molecular Computers and DNA as Data Storage – DNA can store information, but complete control and understanding of this technology are still developing.

Quantum Teleportation – The phenomenon of teleporting information at a quantum level is real, but its fundamental nature and potential uses remain enigmatic.

Biocompatible Neural Implants – Neurotechnology now enables implants to support brain functions, though long-term effects are still unknown.

Augmented Reality (AR) and Its Effect on the Mind – AR technology alters perceptions of reality, yet its long-term psychological and social impacts are not fully understood.

Section: Mistakes That Led to Discoveries

Penicillin – Alexander Fleming accidentally discovered penicillin when he left a petri dish open, and mold developed, killing the surrounding bacteria.

X-Rays – Wilhelm Röntgen discovered X-rays by accident when he noticed a mysterious glow on a fluorescent screen during radiation experiments.

Microwave Oven – Percy Spencer noticed a candy bar melting in his pocket while working with a magnetron, leading to the invention of the microwave.

Post-it Notes – Spencer Silver developed a weak adhesive initially deemed useless, but it later became perfect for sticky notes.

Mauveine Dye – William Perkin, trying to synthesize a malaria drug, accidentally created a purple dye that became fashionable.

Super Glue – Harry Coover created a strong adhesive accidentally while researching optical materials; the substance was too sticky for his project but ideal as a glue.

Teflon – Roy Plunkett stumbled upon Teflon during research on refrigerant gases, later used for non-stick coatings.

Velcro – George de Mestral, while on a walk, noticed how plant burrs clung to his clothes, inspiring him to create Velcro fasteners.

Citric Acid – Carl Scheele discovered citric acid by accident during unrelated chemical reactions, aiding the food industry.

Safety Glass – Edouard Benedictus invented safety glass when he accidentally dropped a cellulose-coated flask that didn't shatter.

Matches – John Walker discovered matches by mixing chemicals that ignited when rubbed.

Plastic (Bakelite) – Leo Baekeland, seeking a shellac alternative, accidentally created Bakelite, the first synthetic plastic.

Insulin – Frederick Banting discovered insulin while studying the pancreas, revolutionizing diabetes treatment.

Coca-Cola – John Pemberton accidentally created Coca-Cola while experimenting with a pain remedy, resulting in the drink's unique taste.

Hubble's Law – Edwin Hubble discovered the universe's expansion through a mistaken analysis of galactic distances, leading to the redshift discovery.

Viagra – Initially studied as a treatment for hypertension, Viagra's unexpected effect led to its use for erectile dysfunction.

Saccharin – Constantin Fahlberg discovered saccharin by accident after forgetting to wash his hands, noticing a sweet taste.

Vulcanized Rubber – Charles Goodyear accidentally discovered vulcanization when a rubber-sulfur mixture fell on a hot stove.

Stainless Steel – Harry Brearley discovered stainless steel while researching corrosion-resistant alloys, accidentally creating a rust-proof metal.

Styrofoam – Dow Chemical discovered Styrofoam accidentally while researching insulating materials, resulting in a lightweight, insulating material.

Section: Lost Inventions

Greek Fire – Used by the Byzantines, this incendiary weapon could burn even on water. Its exact formula was lost, leaving it shrouded in mystery.

Damascus Steel – Known for its incredibly sharp blades, the unique forging process behind Damascus steel was lost, making it difficult to replicate its properties.

Roman Concrete (Opus Caementicium) – This durable Roman concrete allowed structures to endure for centuries, but the full recipe was forgotten over time.

Antikythera Mechanism – Although this ancient mechanical "computer" was found, the knowledge of complex calculation devices was lost for many centuries.

Archimedes' War Machines – Ancient texts describe advanced war machines like Archimedes' "burning mirrors," yet the knowledge of these inventions vanished over time.

Mirrors Made of Metal Alloys – Ancient Egyptians and Babylonians crafted metal-alloy mirrors, but the exact method of production remains unknown.

Ancient Water Clocks – The intricate water clocks used in ancient Egypt and Greece were lost along with the precision technology needed to recreate them.

Flexible Glass – According to Roman legend, an inventor created glass that would return to shape after being dented; the process disappeared without a trace.

Silphium – Medicinal and Culinary Herb – Highly valued by the Greeks and Romans as a spice and medicinal herb, Silphium became extinct, and its uses were lost.

Murrhine Glass – This ancient Roman glassware was known for its durability and luster but was lost after the fall of Rome.

Incan Stone-Building Techniques – The Incas built large stone structures without mortar, a skill that remains a mystery to modern engineers.

Pompeii Fresco Technique – The vibrant, long-lasting colors in Pompeii's frescoes suggest an advanced technique that was lost after the city's destruction.

Polished Gold and Silver Mirrors of the Maya – The Maya crafted high-quality mirrors from polished metals, but the method for this fine polishing has been lost.

Alkahest (Universal Solvent) – Alchemists believed in a solvent that could dissolve any material, though it only exists in legend and ancient writings.

Iron-Fortified Milk of the Romans – Romans fortified milk with iron as one of the earliest mineral supplements, a method forgotten for centuries.

Piri Reis Map – This map created by an Ottoman cartographer depicted lands unknown to explorers of the time, and the details of its creation remain a mystery.

Self-Irrigating Gardens of Babylon – The Hanging Gardens of Babylon, if real, had advanced irrigation techniques that modern science has not yet replicated.

Egyptian Mummification Oils – Egyptians used a special oil to prevent decomposition in mummified bodies, but the exact formula remains unknown.

Ancient Chinese Textile Pressing – Ancient China developed techniques to press silk and cotton with unmatched quality, which was later lost.

Automated Mechanisms of Heron of Alexandria – Heron invented automatic doors and hydraulic systems, yet many of these ingenious devices did not survive through history.

Chapter 7: Nature and Geology

Section: Volcanic Phenomena

Fissure Eruptions – When lava flows from long cracks in the Earth's crust, creating vast lava fields, as seen in Iceland.

Caldera – A massive volcanic collapse following an eruption, like the Yellowstone Caldera, where magma pressure release leaves a large depression.

Volcanic Lava Lakes – Rare pools of liquid lava within craters of active volcanoes, such as Erta Ale in Ethiopia.

Explosive Eruption – A violent eruption ejecting material with force, often forming ash clouds, as in the eruption of Mount St. Helens.

Strombolian Eruption – Characterized by regular explosions of pyroclastic material and lava fountains, like those at Stromboli volcano in Italy.

Hawaiian-style Eruption – Calm, fluid lava flows spreading over large areas, typical of shield volcanoes like Mauna Loa in Hawaii.

Volcanic Gases – Volcanoes emit gases like sulfur dioxide, carbon dioxide, and water vapor, which can impact the atmosphere and climate.

Lahar – Volcanic mudflows made of ash, earth, and water, rushing down mountainsides with destructive force.

Pyroclastic Flow – Hot gases and volcanic materials racing down slopes at high speed, devastating everything in their path.

Fumaroles – Openings in the Earth's surface that release volcanic gases; these vents often emit steam and other gases, even after volcanic activity wanes.

Geysers and Hot Springs – Geothermal activity heats underground water, leading to eruptions of hot water and steam, as seen in Yellowstone National Park.

Pumice – A lightweight, porous volcanic rock formed from quickly cooled frothy magma, so light it can float on water.

Volcanic Bombs – Large rock fragments hurled during eruptions, posing significant danger to surrounding areas.

Volcanic Tsunamis – Underwater eruptions or partial collapses of volcanoes into the ocean can trigger tsunamis, as with the Krakatau eruption.

Rhyolite Lava Domes – Formed from thick, viscous lava, these domes appear on volcano summits post-eruption, such as Mount St. Helens.

Basalt Lava Flows – Extensive basalt lava flows that cover large areas, forming vast formations like the Columbia Plateau in the USA.

Volcanic Ash – Microscopic particles of volcanic glass released during eruptions, which can linger in the atmosphere and influence the climate.

Volcanic Islands – Formed from underwater volcanic eruptions that rise above sea level, as in the cases of Iceland and Hawaii.

Crater Lakes – Lakes filling the craters of extinct volcanoes, such as Crater Lake in the USA, formed after a volcanic collapse.

Volcanic Diamonds – Diamonds can be brought to the surface by kimberlite eruptions, transporting minerals from Earth's deep layers.

Section: Mysterious Lakes and Rivers

Lake Natron, Tanzania – The lake's highly saline and alkaline water can naturally mummify deceased animals, coating them in a mineral-rich crust.

Red Lake, Spain – Known for its intense red color, this lake contains high levels of iron and sulfuric acid, making it both uniquely hued and toxic.

Loch Ness, Scotland – Famous for the legend of the Loch Ness Monster, known as Nessie; its existence remains unconfirmed despite numerous searches.

Caño Cristales River, Colombia – Known as the "River of Five Colors," its hues of red, yellow, green, and blue are due to algae and specific minerals.

Roopkund Lake, India – Also known as the "Skeleton Lake," it contains hundreds of ancient human remains, whose origins remain a mystery.

Ucayali River, Peru – A river in the Amazon jungle, filled with submerged ruins and artifacts from pre-colonial civilizations.

Lake Balkhash, Kazakhstan – A lake with both freshwater and saline sections, though the exact cause of this phenomenon is still not fully understood.

Lake Hillier, Australia – A pink lake with color believed to be due to specific algae and bacteria, though the exact cause remains partially unknown.

Whanganui River, New Zealand – The only river in the world legally recognized as a person, it holds special cultural significance to the Māori.

Crater Lake, USA – The deepest lake in the USA, formed by a volcanic eruption; its unusually clear water remains a scientific mystery.

Lake Retba, Senegal – Known as the "Pink Lake," it has a high salt content, and its color changes from pink to red due to bacteria.

Lake Titicaca, Peru and Bolivia – The world's highest navigable lake, surrounded by legends of sunken cities and the Incan civilization.

Double River, Colombia – A unique river flowing in two channels simultaneously, with waters of different temperatures and minerals.

Lake Van, Turkey – A salty lake with high sodium levels and unique bacteria; some parts change color depending on the season.

Tinto River, Spain – This red river contains heavy metals, and its unique microorganisms can survive in its highly acidic environment.

Lake Vostok, Antarctica – A massive subglacial lake isolated for millions of years, possibly harboring unknown forms of life.

Shambhala River, Russia – A legendary river said to "disappear" and change course, making it difficult to locate.

Lake Maracaibo, Venezuela – Known for frequent electric storms, it's one of the most active storm areas on Earth.

Lake Baikal, Russia – The world's deepest and one of the oldest lakes, home to unique species, including freshwater seals.

River of Lakes (Río de los Lagos), Chile – A river that vanishes and reappears in different locations due to shifting groundwater levels, puzzling hydrologists.

Section: Extraordinary Mountains and Rock Formations

Uluru (Ayers Rock), Australia – This massive red monolith changes colors depending on the time of day and season and is considered sacred by the Aboriginal people.

Table Mountains, Poland – Known for their flat tops and maze-like formations, these sandstone mountains were shaped by erosion over millions of years.

Giant's Causeway, Northern Ireland – A unique formation of thousands of hexagonal basalt columns formed by volcanic activity, steeped in local legend.

Grand Canyon, USA – A vast canyon carved by the Colorado River, exposing geological layers millions of years old.

Tianzi Mountains, China – These tall, slender rock pillars rise vertically, inspiring the landscape of the movie Avatar.

Fairy Chimneys, Turkey – Located in Cappadocia, these volcanic rock formations resemble towers and spires sculpted by erosion.

Monument Valley, USA – Impressive red sandstone formations on Navajo land that symbolize the iconic landscapes of the American Wild West.

Torghatten, Norway – Known for a hole that runs through the mountain, which, according to legend, was made by a troll's arrow.

Gates of Hell, Turkmenistan – A massive gas crater that has been burning since the 1970s, giving the appearance of an eternal fire.

Mount Roraima, Venezuela/Brazil/Guyana – Known as a "tepui," this table-top mountain has sheer cliffs and flat summits, creating an otherworldly landscape.

Wave Rock, Australia – This 46-foot-high rock formation resembles a wave frozen in time, shaped by water and wind erosion.

Wieliczka Salt Mine, Poland – An underground complex of salt chambers, corridors, and sculptures carved by miners over centuries.

North Gates, Canada – Towering formations near Hudson Bay that resemble large walls and columns.

Chocolate Hills, Philippines – These dome-shaped hills turn brown during the dry season, earning them the name "Chocolate Hills."

Crooked Forest, Poland – A mysterious forest where the trees grow with sharply curved trunks, leaving scientists puzzled.

Arches National Park, USA – Located in Utah, this park is home to hundreds of natural stone arches formed by erosion.

Enchanted City (Ciudad Encantada), Spain – Rock formations resembling castles, animals, and other shapes, created by natural erosion.

Bryce Canyon, USA – Known for its hoodoos, tall spire-shaped rock formations that create a striking red-orange landscape.

Percé Rock, Canada – A large rock formation in the Gulf of Saint Lawrence with a natural arch that has withstood erosion over centuries.

Stone Forest (Shilin), China – A unique landscape of vertical rock formations resembling a forest of petrified trees.

Section: Earth as a Living Organism

Gaia Hypothesis – Proposed by James Lovelock, this theory suggests that Earth and all its components operate as a self-regulating organism, maintaining environmental balance.

Biogeochemical Cycles – Processes like the water, carbon, and nitrogen cycles allow essential chemical flows for life, functioning similarly to metabolic cycles in living organisms.

Atmospheric Regulation – Plants producing oxygen, microorganisms absorbing methane, and oceans taking in CO_2 all support atmospheric stability, akin to respiratory processes in living beings.

Role of Microorganisms – Microorganisms like soil bacteria and ocean plankton act like Earth's "organs," processing organic matter and sustaining life.

Oceans as Earth's "Circulatory System" – Ocean currents transport heat and nutrients, redistributing resources throughout the planet like blood circulation in an organism.

Temperature Equilibrium – Earth's natural mechanisms regulate temperature, such as ice reflecting sunlight, akin to how organisms maintain internal temperature.

Volcanoes as Earth's "Pores" – Volcanoes release heat and gases from within, facilitating the cycle of elements and maintaining balance, similar to excretion in organisms.

Photosynthesis and Earth's "Nutrition" – Through photosynthesis, plants convert solar energy into biological energy, essentially "feeding" the planet.

Forests as Earth's "Lungs" – Forests, especially tropical ones, absorb carbon dioxide and produce oxygen, just like lungs in a living organism.

Tides as Earth's "Pulse" – Ocean tides, driven by lunar gravity, mimic a rhythmic pulse that affects coastal ecosystems' stability.

Tree Root Systems as Communication Networks – Tree roots, especially in forests, collaborate with mycorrhizal fungi to form a "plant internet," allowing for nutrient and information exchange.

Glaciers as Water Reservoirs – Glaciers store vast amounts of freshwater, akin to an organism storing reserves for survival during tough times.

Deserts as Earth's "Skin" – Deserts function as protective barriers, limiting erosion and regulating wind, similar to how skin protects an organism.

Earth's "Disasters" as Renewal Mechanisms – Events like wildfires, earthquakes, and volcanic eruptions can renew ecosystems, mirroring how organisms repair after injury.

Soil Nutrient Cycling – Soil acts like Earth's "digestive system," processing organic matter and providing nutrients to plants.

Diverse Biomes as "Organs" of the Planet – Different ecosystems, such as forests, oceans, and deserts, serve unique functions that complement one another, much like organs in a body.

Regeneration After Natural Disasters – Earth has a capacity for self-repair after events like volcanic eruptions and meteor strikes, akin to wound healing.

Earth as a Closed System – Earth operates as a closed system where resources are recycled, with a relatively constant amount of matter, much like an organism.

Clouds and Evaporation as Earth's "Excretory System" – The processes of evaporation and condensation act as a way to recycle and cleanse water, similar to excretory functions in organisms.

Earth's Energy Balance – Earth receives solar energy and radiates heat into space, allowing temperature stability, comparable to energy metabolism in organisms.

Section: The Rock Cycle

Formation of Igneous Rocks – The rock cycle begins when hot magma from Earth's interior cools, forming igneous rocks, such as granite (forming underground) or basalt (forming on the surface).

Formation of Plutonic and Volcanic Rocks – When magma cools deep underground, it forms plutonic rocks; when it erupts to the surface, it forms volcanic rocks.

Weathering and Erosion – Igneous rocks on the surface undergo physical, chemical, and biological weathering, breaking down into smaller particles.

Sediment Transport – Erosion carries rock particles through water, wind, or ice, transporting sediment to rivers, seas, or lakes.

Sedimentation – Sediments accumulate in layers in bodies of water and other areas, marking the start of the formation of sedimentary rocks.

Compaction of Sediments – Under the weight of overlying layers, sediments compact, becoming denser and more ready for transformation into sedimentary rocks.

Cementation of Sediments – Minerals dissolved in water fill gaps between sediment particles, forming solid sedimentary rocks like sandstone and limestone.

Formation of Sedimentary Rocks – Sedimentary rocks, formed from compacted and cemented sediments, retain layered structures and often contain fossils.

Metamorphism – Igneous and sedimentary rocks transform into metamorphic rocks, such as marble (from limestone) or gneiss (from granite), under high pressure and temperature.

Physical and Chemical Transformation of Rocks – Under extreme conditions, minerals in rocks change their structure and composition, creating metamorphic rocks with new properties.

Folding and Uplifting – Tectonic movements apply pressure to rocks, leading to folding, uplifting, and the formation of mountain ranges.

Uplift – Bringing Rocks to the Surface – Tectonic processes push deeply buried rocks to the surface, where they undergo further weathering and transformation.

Recycling of Metamorphic Rocks – Once at the surface, metamorphic rocks experience weathering and erosion, restarting the cycle.

Soil Formation – Weathered and eroded rocks break down to form soil, which supports terrestrial ecosystems.

Subduction and Material Recycling – Tectonic plates with sediments and rocks are pulled into Earth's interior through subduction, where they melt and become part of new magma.

Magma Formation from Melting Rocks – In subduction zones, rocks subjected to high pressure and heat melt, forming new magma.

Volcanism as Part of the Rock Cycle – Newly formed magma can erupt to the surface through volcanic eruptions, creating new igneous rocks.

Dependence of Sedimentary Rocks on the Water Cycle – Processes essential to sedimentary rock formation, like erosion and sedimentation, are driven by the water cycle in rivers, seas, and lakes.

Silicate and Carbonate Rocks as Carbon Storage – Rocks like limestone store significant amounts of carbon, impacting the global carbon cycle and climate.

The Endless Rock Cycle – The rock cycle is an ongoing process that spans millions of years, preserving the circulation of materials within the lithosphere and supporting geological balance.

Section 8: Food Curiosities

Section: Foods with Surprising Flavors

Durian – A tropical fruit from Southeast Asia with an extremely pungent smell but a creamy, sweet flavor, reminiscent of a mix of mango and vanilla.

Hákarl (fermented shark) – An Icelandic delicacy made from fermented shark meat, with a strong ammonia smell and a milder taste, similar to certain types of cheese.

Japanese Persimmons (Kaki) – These fruits are astringent when unripe, but after ripening, they become very sweet and tender, resembling flavors of pumpkin and honey.

Jackfruit – Raw jackfruit tastes like a blend of mango and pineapple, but when cooked, its texture and flavor are similar to chicken.

Salty Licorice (Salmiakki) – Popular in Scandinavia, this black licorice has an intensely salty flavor, surprising for those used to the sweet variety.

Casu Marzu Cheese – A Sardinian sheep's milk cheese with live larvae, known for its intense, tangy flavor, cherished by fans of bold tastes.

Umeboshi (Japanese pickled plums) – Very sour and salty, resembling the taste of fermented lemons, commonly enjoyed with rice.

Black Garlic – After fermentation, garlic becomes soft and sweet, with a flavor profile similar to balsamic vinegar and plums.

Kimchi – A Korean fermented cabbage with a tangy, spicy flavor and distinctive aroma resulting from the fermentation process.

Miso – A fermented soybean paste with a rich umami flavor, reminiscent of nuts and roasted meats, often used in soups and sauces.

Tamarillo – A fruit with a sweet-tart flavor that combines notes of tomato, citrus, and passion fruit, popular in New Zealand.

Century Eggs – A Chinese delicacy of preserved eggs with a creamy texture and slightly ammonia-like taste, featuring a unique aroma.

Mangosteen – A tropical fruit with a surprisingly sweet and tangy flavor, tasting like a blend of pineapple, peach, and strawberry.

Roquefort Cheese – A French blue cheese known for its salty-sharp taste and characteristic blue mold aroma, surprising for many.

Achiote (Annatto) – A seasoning with a mildly sweet, slightly peppery taste and nutty undertones, known for its vibrant orange color.

Durian Coffee – Popular in Southeast Asia, a coffee that combines durian fruit's aroma with coffee notes, a surprising taste for many.

Wasabi Ice Cream – A Japanese treat combining sweet ice cream with a spicy, wasabi-like kick, creating a unique flavor experience.

Watermelon Pickles – Popular in the United States, pickles made from watermelon rinds offer a mix of fruity sweetness with sour brine.

Natto (fermented soybeans) – A traditional Japanese dish with a sticky texture and a strong, cheese-like flavor, evoking mixed reactions.

Civet Coffee (Kopi Luwak) – Produced from beans eaten and excreted by civets, resulting in a smooth, slightly caramelized flavor, surprising even seasoned coffee drinkers.

Section: Food in World Cultures

Sushi, Japan – Known globally, this dish of raw fish and rice was initially a method for preserving fish and is now a symbol of Japanese cuisine.

Paella, Spain – A traditional Valencian dish of rice, seafood, meat, and vegetables, symbolizing Mediterranean abundance and rich flavors.

Kimchi, South Korea – Spicy, fermented cabbage that serves not only as a side dish but also as a symbol of health and strength in Korean culture.

Biryani, India – A fragrant rice dish with spices, meat, or vegetables, that embodies the diversity and rich use of spices in Indian cuisine.

Couscous, Morocco – A North African dish made from couscous grains, symbolizing hospitality and often served during communal meals.

Falafel, Middle East – Fried chickpea or fava bean balls symbolizing simplicity and vegetarian traditions in Middle Eastern cuisine.

Haggis, Scotland – A dish of sheep's offal, spices, and oats, cooked in the animal's stomach, representing Scottish tradition and national holidays.

Poutine, Canada – Fries topped with cheese curds and gravy, symbolizing the fusion of French and English culinary traditions in Quebec.

Feijoada, Brazil – A black bean and meat stew, Brazil's national dish, often enjoyed at family gatherings.

Pho, Vietnam – A flavorful broth with rice noodles and herbs, representing the simplicity and flavor combinations of Vietnamese cuisine.

Tacos, Mexico – Corn tortillas filled with various ingredients, from meats to vegetables, embodying the diversity of Mexican street food and cuisine.

Ceviche, Peru – Raw fish marinated in lime juice, onions, and spices, symbolizing freshness and the variety of South American flavors.

Fufu, West Africa – A thick paste made from yams, cassava, or plantains, eaten with stews, integral to West African culinary culture.

Pizza, Italy – Originating in Naples, pizza is now an international symbol of Italian creativity, cuisine, and simplicity.

Baklava, Turkey – A filo pastry with nuts and honey, popular in the Middle East, symbolizing richness and the sweetness of life.

Biltong, South Africa – Dried, spiced meat that's the South African version of jerky, symbolizing hunting traditions and food preservation.

Churros, Spain & Latin America – Fried dough pastries often served with chocolate, popular as breakfast or during festivals.

Sauerbraten, Germany – Marinated beef roast served with dumplings or cabbage, representing German home cooking and culinary traditions.

Pavlova, New Zealand & Australia – A dessert made with meringue, cream, and fruit, created in honor of Russian ballerina Anna Pavlova, cherished in both countries.

Dango, Japan – Sweet rice flour dumplings on a stick, often served at festivals and holidays, embodying Japanese tradition and simplicity.

Section: History of Culinary Customs

Ancient feasting in Mesopotamia – Feasts to honor gods and rulers were known as early as ancient Mesopotamia, featuring meat, fish, bread, and abundant alcohol.

Wine rituals in ancient Greece – In Greece, symposiums or wine gatherings were occasions for philosophical discussions, where wine was diluted with water as a symbol of moderation.

Early fast food in ancient Rome – Roman thermopolia were the first "hot food bars," serving quick meals like stews and bread for people on the go.

Chinese tea ceremony – Dating back over a thousand years, this tradition of tea consumption reflects respect for nature and the relaxing aspects of life.

European Renaissance banquets – Spectacular events where nobles enjoyed game, spices, and sugar, then a rare luxury.

Drinking chocolate among the Maya and Aztecs – Chocolate, considered a drink of the gods, was served cold with spices in Mesoamerican cultures.

Medieval culinary superstitions – Europeans in the Middle Ages believed garlic warded off evil spirits, and herbs like rosemary protected against illness.

Japanese ritual of burying plant remnants – For centuries, Japanese farmers buried plant remnants to enrich soil, a precursor to today's composting culture.

The art of food presentation in China – Chinese cuisine emphasized beautiful plating, incorporating yin and yang and flavor harmony.

Bread-sharing tradition in European cultures – In Europe, bread has long symbolized family unity and hospitality, and sharing it embodies warmth and welcome.

French multi-course dining – In the 17th century, France introduced structured meals with appetizers, main courses, and desserts, enhancing dining aesthetics and encouraging leisurely feasts.

Fat Thursday and Mardi Gras – Celebrated before Lent in Poland and other countries, these are days for enjoying rich, sweet foods in farewell to abundance.

First soups in clay pots – In ancient Japan and China, soups were simmered in clay pots, reflecting respect for ingredients and the art of slow cooking.

Arabian spice traditions – Medieval Arabs mastered spicing foods with cinnamon, cardamom, and saffron, valued for both taste and health benefits.

Sushi as a preservation method – Originally, sushi preserved fish through fermentation in rice and salt, before evolving into the fresh dish we know today.

Samurai dining customs – Samurai observed strict eating practices, focusing on simple meals like rice, vegetables, and fish to maintain discipline and strength.

Ethiopian communal eating from a single bowl – Eating together from one bowl symbolizes community and intimacy, a longstanding tradition in Ethiopia's agrarian society.

Italian dining as a family affair – Italian food and customs emphasize family gatherings, with meals serving as a way to maintain social bonds.

Bread and salt welcome in Slavic culture – Bread and salt symbolize hospitality in Slavic cultures and are used in greetings and important celebrations.

Modern molecular gastronomy – Today, molecular gastronomy blends tradition with innovation, using scientific techniques to explore new textures and tastes.

Section: Culinary Art of Past Eras

Mesopotamian cuisine – The earliest recipes originated in Mesopotamia, featuring fish, bread, and vegetables seasoned with aromatic herbs and spices.

Ancient Egyptian cuisine – Egyptians enjoyed bread, onions, and beer; their feasts included meats, wild birds, and fish, often adorned with rich sauces and honey.

Greek cuisine – symposium – In ancient Greece, symposia were popular gatherings where wine, seafood, olives, and cheese were served, and food accompanied philosophical discussions.

Ancient Roman cuisine – Romans relished extravagant feasts with dishes like garum (fish sauce), oysters, eels, and exotic fruits, along with nut and honey cakes.

Medieval cuisine – game and spices – In medieval Europe, royal banquets served game, fish, and poultry, lavishly seasoned with costly spices like cinnamon and cloves.

Renaissance cooking – Renaissance cuisine embraced herbal flavors and experimented with New World spices, with dishes often garnished with edible flowers.

Baroque royal banquets – In the 17th century, European courts favored lavish spreads, including roasted swans, peacocks, and decorative wine fountains.

Japanese tea ceremony – In Japan, the tea ceremony developed as a ritual intertwined with Zen philosophy, emphasizing simplicity and aesthetic minimalism.

Mongolian cooking methods on hunts – During Genghis Khan's era, Mongolian warriors prepared simple, energy-rich foods like meat and grains that could be easily cooked on the go.

The Maya and Aztecs – chocolate as the drink of the gods – In pre-Columbian America, chocolate was a bitter, spiced drink representing strength and wealth, often reserved for the elite.

Chinese art of steaming and braising – Ancient Chinese cooking used steaming and braising techniques, often with a wok, creating a cuisine focused on balanced flavors and herbs.

Arab cuisine – influenced by the Silk Road – Arabs developed a cuisine rich in spices from the Far East, like turmeric, saffron, and cinnamon, crafting fragrant dishes of meat and rice.

Tradition of winter food storage in Northern Europe – In Scandinavia and northern regions, food preservation through smoking and salting became essential to survive harsh winters, shaping the region's cuisine.

French haute cuisine in the 18th century – French culinary art became highly refined, with a focus on delicate flavors, subtle sauces, and elegant presentation.

Venetian feasts in the Renaissance – With access to trade routes, Venetian cuisine flourished with spices, seafood, and exotic ingredients, creating a unique, cosmopolitan flavor.

Modern Italian pasta and pizza – In Italy, the introduction of tomatoes led to dishes like pasta and pizza, which quickly gained popularity nationwide.

Slavic traditions of fermenting – In Slavic cultures, fermenting vegetables like cabbage and cucumbers became a staple, allowing for winter storage.

Incan cuisine in Peru – The Inca cultivated thousands of potato and corn varieties, creating a highland-based cuisine that relied on natural ingredients like quinoa and fish from Lake Titicaca.

Imperial Ottoman cuisine – The Ottoman Empire's cuisine blended Asian and Middle Eastern flavors, with tables laden with lamb, rice, and fruits.

Victorian feasts and snacks – In Victorian Britain, afternoon tea and refined snacks, such as sandwiches, biscuits, and cakes, became fashionable and were served on elegant tableware.

Section: Animals in Human Cuisine

Cultural meat taboo in India – In Hinduism, cows are considered sacred, so eating beef is largely prohibited, with diets primarily based on vegetables and legumes.

Pork in Middle Eastern cuisine – In both Judaism and Islam, pork is deemed unclean and is forbidden, significantly shaping the culinary traditions of the region.

Beef as a status symbol in the USA – Beef dishes like steaks and burgers have become icons of American cuisine, particularly representing prosperity in the South and Midwest.

Fish in Japanese cuisine – Japan is renowned for its tradition of consuming fish, such as in sushi and sashimi, reflecting a culture deeply connected to the sea.

Insects in Southeast Asian cuisine – In countries like Thailand and Cambodia, insects such as crickets, larvae, and scorpions are popular protein-rich delicacies.

Game meat in Scandinavian cuisine – Traditionally, Scandinavians consume reindeer, moose, and wild boar, an adaptation to the harsh climate and reliance on local resources.

Sheep and lamb in Greek cuisine – With sheep farming common in Greece, lamb and mutton are staples, especially during holidays like Easter.

Duck in Chinese cuisine – Peking duck from Beijing is famous for its crispy skin and intricate preparation, representing a hallmark of Chinese culinary tradition.

Snails in French cuisine – Known as escargot, snails prepared with garlic and butter are a refined delicacy in France.

Goats in African and Middle Eastern cuisine – Goats are popular in Africa and the Middle East, with their meat often served on special occasions as a delicacy.

Rabbit in Spanish cuisine – Rabbit is a key ingredient in traditional dishes like Valencian paella and is a common meat choice in Spain.

Frogs as delicacies in France and Asia – Frog legs are enjoyed in France and countries like Vietnam, valued for their delicate flavor.

Lamb in Middle Eastern cuisine – In countries like Turkey, lamb is a central ingredient, commonly grilled, roasted, or cooked on a spit.

Octopus and squid in Mediterranean cuisine – Mediterranean countries, including Italy and Greece, serve octopus and squid grilled or fried.

Camel in Arab cuisine – Camel is served during important events in the Middle East as a symbol of hospitality and abundance.

Herring in Scandinavian and Russian cuisine – Pickled and salted herring is a staple in Scandinavia and Russia, symbolizing regional seafood traditions.

Kangaroo in Australian cuisine – In Australia, kangaroo meat is an eco-friendly, lean choice, though not as widely consumed as other meats.

Turkey as an American tradition – Turkey is central to Thanksgiving in the U.S., embodying family traditions.

Trout in Alpine cuisine – In the Alps, especially in Switzerland and Austria, trout is popular, thanks to mountain rivers and lakes.

Wild game in French cuisine – Wild game birds like quail and pheasant are part of traditional French hunting cuisine, celebrated for their rich flavors.

Chapter 9: The World of Science

Section: The Physics of Everyday Life

Friction in daily life – Friction allows us to walk, brake cars, and operate many devices like zippers and pens.

Gravity as a fundamental force – Gravity causes objects to fall and keeps us anchored to Earth's surface, allowing stable movement and living conditions.

Atmospheric pressure and boiling water – Air pressure affects the boiling point of water, which is why, for example, water boils at a lower temperature at high altitudes.

Mirror reflection – The phenomenon of light reflection lets us see our reflection in mirrors, a principle also used in periscopes and binoculars.

Capillarity and water absorption in plants – Capillary action enables water to move up through plants, allowing them to draw moisture from the soil and transport it to the leaves.

Lever mechanics – Levers reduce the force needed to perform tasks and are found in scissors, pliers, and seesaws.

Centripetal and centrifugal forces – Centrifugal force in a washing machine pushes water out of clothes during the spin cycle.

Magnetism and magnetic attraction – Magnets attract iron objects, used in household items like fridge magnets, toys, and office or workshop tools.

Doppler effect and sirens – When an ambulance siren approaches, the sound pitch increases, and as it moves away, it decreases; the Doppler effect is also used in radar technology.

Glass and light refraction – Water and glass bend light passing through them, which is the basis for glasses, lenses, and microscopes.

Elasticity of materials – Elasticity lets materials return to their original shape, useful in items like erasers, springs, and balls.

Thermal expansion – Materials expand with heat, a principle applied in bridge construction with special joints to allow for stretching and contracting.

Heat transfer and insulation – Heat flows from warmer to cooler areas, which is harnessed in building insulation, thermoses, and winter clothing.

Fluid and gas pressure – The principle of fluid pressure is used in syringes, spray bottles, and car hydraulic lifts.

Increasing pressure with diving depth – As divers go deeper underwater, pressure increases, affecting their bodies and requiring safety precautions.

Thermal conductivity of metals – Metals conduct heat, allowing us to cook and heat efficiently; used in pots, pans, and radiators.

Pendulum motion – Pendulums are used in clocks and serve as a model for wave motion in physics.

Non-wetting surfaces – Lotus leaves' non-wetting surface properties inspire modern waterproof technology, such as rain-resistant clothing and car coatings.

Principle of balance – This principle explains that a balanced object remains stable, foundational in bridge design, ladders, and support structures.

Evaporation and sweating – Evaporation helps release heat from the skin through sweating, a natural cooling process for the body.

Section: Biology We Never Knew

Extremophile bacteria – These organisms survive in extreme environments like hot springs and deep-sea vents, enduring conditions where most life would perish, expanding our understanding of possible life habitats.

Bioluminescence – Organisms such as fireflies, jellyfish, and deep-sea fish emit light to communicate, hunt, or ward off predators, showcasing nature's surprising adaptations.

Human microbiome – Our bodies host trillions of bacteria that influence health, digestion, and immunity, making them an essential part of our overall function.

Inter-species symbiosis – From cleaner fish on sharks to bacteria in our guts, interspecies dependencies are far more common and complex than previously thought.

Forest communication networks (Wood Wide Web) – Trees and fungi create mycorrhizal networks that allow plants to communicate and share nutrients, revealing a hidden world of forest cooperation.

Epigenetics – Research shows that our environment and lifestyle can influence gene expression without altering DNA itself, revolutionizing our understanding of genetics.

Limb regeneration in animals – Some animals, like salamanders and starfish, can regenerate lost limbs or organs, opening new paths for regenerative medicine.

Photosynthesis without sunlight – Deep-sea organisms use chemical energy instead of sunlight to produce food, reshaping our ideas of where and how life can thrive.

Phenotypic plasticity – Some species, such as geckos and chameleons, can change physical traits in response to environmental shifts, showcasing remarkable adaptability.

Mitochondrial transplantation – Some cells can transfer mitochondria to others, affecting tissue repair and immunity.

Life without oxygen – Discovery of multicellular organisms in anaerobic environments expands the possibilities for extraterrestrial life.

Biomimetics – nature-inspired technology – By studying birds' flight, spider silk, or lotus leaves, scientists are developing new materials and technologies inspired by nature.

Electricity-producing bacteria – Certain bacteria generate electrons, opening the door to biological power sources.

Apoptosis – programmed cell death – Apoptosis is a process where cells self-destruct to protect the organism, playing a crucial role in development and health.

Tardigrades and resilience to extreme conditions – Tardigrades (water bears) survive desiccation, radiation, and extreme temperatures, inspiring research on resilience.

Hydrothermal vent ecosystems on ocean floors – Unique ecosystems form around hydrothermal vents, hosting unknown organisms that thrive without sunlight.

Memory storage in DNA – Research on cellular memory suggests that experiences can influence future generations through changes in DNA structure.

Life in cryoconite holes on glaciers – Microorganisms survive in glacier micro-depressions, adapted to life in ice and freezing temperatures.

Biological immortality in Turritopsis dohrnii jellyfish – This jellyfish can revert to an earlier stage of development, potentially escaping death from natural causes.

Stem cells and their regenerative potential – Stem cells can transform into any cell type in the body, revolutionizing regenerative and transplant medicine.

Section: The Chemical Mysteries

Chemical composition of Venus's atmosphere – The atmosphere of Venus is rich in sulfuric acid and carbon dioxide, creating extreme conditions and a mysterious greenhouse effect, one of the strongest in the Solar System.

The peculiar property of water – Water expands when it freezes, a rare property that allows life to thrive in cold environments under protective ice layers.

Liquid crystals – These materials exist between solid and liquid states, altering properties with temperature and electricity, and are used in LCD displays.

Gold dissolvable in aqua regia – Despite its durability, gold can dissolve in a mixture of hydrochloric and nitric acid, known as aqua regia, captivating chemists for centuries.

Phenomenon of non-Newtonian fluids – Substances like cornstarch mixed with water change viscosity under force, enabling unique behaviors like "walking on water" under specific conditions.

Catalysts – Catalysts speed up chemical reactions without being consumed, playing vital roles in industry and biological processes.

The mystery of fluorescent proteins – Some organisms, like jellyfish, possess fluorescent proteins that absorb and emit light, a property used in biological research.

Diamond and graphite – two forms of the same element – Both composed of carbon, diamond and graphite exhibit vastly different properties due to their distinct atomic structures.

Self-cleaning fluids – Inspired by lotus leaf structures, some fluids and coatings repel water and dirt, with applications in nanotechnology.

Hydrophobic and hydrophilic surfaces – Hydrophobic surfaces repel water, while hydrophilic surfaces attract it, crucial in the creation of fabrics, glass, and self-cleaning materials.

Exothermic and endothermic reactions – Reactions that release heat (exothermic) or absorb it (endothermic) are used in hot packs and cold compresses.

Protein structure – Proteins, composed of amino acids, derive their function from their 3D structure; misfolded proteins can cause diseases, a mystery in biomedicine.

Chemical properties of mercury – Mercury is the only metal liquid at room temperature, with intriguing physical properties and notable toxicity.

Hydrofluoric acid's reaction with silicon – Hydrofluoric acid can dissolve glass, making it essential in chemistry and microprocessor production.

Oxides with unusual properties – Certain oxides, like aluminum oxide, exhibit both acidic and basic properties, making them invaluable in the chemical industry.

Self-organizing molecules – Under specific conditions, molecules can form structures resembling cells, relevant to studies of the origin of life.

Plasma – the fourth state of matter – Plasma, an ionized gas, is the fourth state of matter found in auroras, lightning, and stars.

Chemical reactions under extreme conditions – Reactions at high pressures and temperatures, such as in Earth's depths, produce minerals unattainable on the surface.

Superconducting substances – Materials that conduct electricity without resistance at low temperatures have promising technological and energy applications.

Cryogenics and low-temperature materials – In extreme cold, materials exhibit unique properties utilized in material science and space exploration.

Section: Geometry and Mathematics in Everyday Life

Symmetry in nature – Symmetry is evident in the shapes of leaves, snowflakes, and butterfly wings, forming the basis of aesthetics and balance in nature.

Geometric shapes in architecture – Triangles, squares, and circles are widely used in construction to enhance structural strength and building aesthetics.

The golden ratio – The golden ratio, approximately 1.618:1, is utilized in art, architecture, and nature to create harmonious and visually pleasing compositions.

Mathematics in cooking and baking – Measuring proportions, weighing ingredients, and calculating volumes are everyday examples of applied mathematics in the kitchen.

Time and clocks – Our lives are regulated by units of time—hours, minutes, and seconds—based on numbers and geometric divisions.

Grid systems in maps and navigation – Maps and GPS systems rely on coordinate grids, distances, and angles for precise location identification.

Mathematics in music – Rhythm and tempo in music are based on fractions, while intervals use mathematical divisions like the octave's proportions.

Accounting and budgeting – Managing budgets and savings involves addition, subtraction, multiplication, and division in daily financial planning.

Geometric figures in interior design – Symmetry and proportions are applied in interior design to achieve aesthetic balance and spatial functionality.

Fractals in nature – Structures like tree branches, coastlines, and snowflakes are examples of fractals, where similar patterns repeat across different scales.

Combinatorics in scheduling and planning – Creating timetables and schedules involves combinations and permutations to determine the most efficient solutions.

Prime numbers in cryptography – Prime numbers are the foundation of many encryption algorithms that secure our online data.

Game theory in negotiations and shopping – Game theory helps optimize decision-making in negotiations and strategic situations aiming for win-win outcomes.

Markov chains in weather forecasting – Probability-based mathematical models like Markov chains aid in predicting weather changes and their likely impacts.

Geometry of shadows and perspective in photography – Composition and light angles in photography use perspective and geometric principles to create realistic or artistic effects.

Mathematics in car design – Designing aerodynamic car shapes relies on geometric calculations to reduce air resistance and improve efficiency.

Statistics in medicine and scientific research – Statistical data analysis helps evaluate drug effectiveness and make evidence-based decisions in medicine.

Proportions and scale in modeling – Creating models of buildings, planes, or trains requires precise calculations of proportions to faithfully replicate originals.

Mathematics in the food industry – Calculations of mass, volume, and quantity are crucial in packaging, storing, and transporting food products.

Geometry in origami art – Origami involves precise folds and angle calculations, demonstrating practical geometry in crafting three-dimensional forms.

Section: Discoveries That Will Shape the Future

CRISPR technology and gene editing – CRISPR allows precise gene modifications, paving the way for curing genetic diseases and advancing personalized medicine.

Artificial intelligence (AI) and machine learning – AI enables automation, data analysis, and forecasting on an unprecedented scale, transforming industries, healthcare, and daily life.

Quantum computing – With computational power surpassing traditional computers, quantum computing could solve complex problems, model molecules, and revolutionize cryptography.

Internet of Things (IoT) – IoT connects everyday devices into networks, improving energy management, home automation, and health monitoring.

Energy from nuclear fusion – Similar to the process powering the Sun, nuclear fusion promises an unlimited, clean energy source, potentially addressing global energy demands.

Lab-grown meat and agriculture – Cultivating meat in laboratories reduces the environmental impact of traditional farming and offers sustainable solutions for a growing population.

Nanotechnology in medicine – Nanoparticles deliver drugs directly to cells, offering more effective treatments for cancer and chronic diseases.

Room-temperature superconducting materials – Superconductors could revolutionize energy transmission by enabling efficient energy storage and minimizing losses.

3D printing of organs – 3D printing technology creates organs using a patient's cells, addressing organ transplant shortages.

New renewable energy sources – Innovations like perovskite solar panels reduce dependence on fossil fuels and support sustainable development.

Brain-computer interfaces – These interfaces enable control of devices through thoughts, empowering individuals with disabilities and creating new ways to interact with technology.

Autonomous vehicles – Self-driving cars promise safer roads, reduced emissions, and transformative travel and transportation methods.

Algae-based biofuels – Algae have potential as a biofuel source, revolutionizing energy industries with an alternative to fossil fuels.

AI-powered diagnostics – AI accelerates medical imaging and test result analysis, aiding in early disease detection and supporting healthcare professionals.

Longer-lasting batteries – Advanced batteries, like lithium-sulfur, store more energy and last longer, crucial for renewable energy storage.

Biodegradable plastics – Advances in eco-friendly materials can significantly reduce plastic pollution and promote sustainable alternatives.

Space exploration and manned missions to Mars – Innovations in rocket technology and space exploration may unlock opportunities for extraterrestrial settlement and research.

The evolution of biomimicry – Nature-inspired innovations, such as self-healing materials, mimic natural regenerative processes and fuel new technological breakthroughs.

Augmented and virtual reality (AR and VR) – These technologies revolutionize education, medicine, and entertainment, introducing immersive ways to interact with digital environments.

Advanced cybersecurity – Progress in quantum cryptography and security technologies strengthens data protection and privacy, countering emerging digital threats.

Chapter 10: Everyday Life

Section: Strange Customs and Superstitions

Collecting broken glass for luck – In countries like Germany, breaking glass before a wedding symbolizes good fortune and protection against misfortune in marriage.

Wearing a red thread on the wrist – In cultures like Jewish and Slavic traditions, a red thread is believed to ward off the "evil eye" and negative energies.

Ban on whistling indoors in Russia – Whistling inside is thought to bring bad luck and cause money to "escape" from the household.

Hiding knives before weddings in Japan – Giving knives as a wedding gift is seen as a symbol of severing relationships, making them an inappropriate present for such occasions.

Cursing at funerals in Greece – Cursing during funerals was believed to ward off evil spirits and protect the deceased's soul from harm.

Breaking plates on New Year's Eve in Denmark – Danes smash plates in front of friends' houses to bring good luck and mark new beginnings.

Hanging a horseshoe above the door – Hanging a horseshoe, particularly in a U-shape, is believed to attract good fortune and guard the home from evil spirits in many cultures.

Spitting three times to ward off bad luck – In Greece and Turkey, people symbolically spit three times to dispel bad luck after hearing unfortunate news.

Avoiding crossed fork and knife – In some countries, crossing a fork and knife on a plate symbolizes conflict and arguments, so this arrangement is avoided.

Keeping fingers crossed for luck – Popular in Europe, crossing fingers or holding thumbs is a gesture of support and sending positive energy.

Placing shoes on a table as a bad omen – Shoes on a table are considered a sign of bad luck in many cultures, foretelling financial or family troubles.

Avoiding the number 4 in Japan – The number 4 sounds similar to the word for "death" in Japanese, making it an inauspicious number, especially in gifts and gatherings.

Leaving crumbs of food for the spirits of the dead – In Mexico, during Día de los Muertos, food is left on altars for the spirits of ancestors believed to return to the living world.

Belief in "lucky days" for weddings in India – In India, astrological calculations are used to select auspicious wedding dates to ensure a harmonious and prosperous marriage.

Salt as protection against evil forces – Sprinkling salt at the threshold of a home or over the shoulder is thought to protect against evil spirits and negative energy.

Walking under ladders as a bad omen – Walking under a ladder is widely avoided, as it is believed to disrupt harmony and bring bad luck.

Crows' cawing as an omen of misfortune – In some cultures, the cawing of crows or ravens is seen as a forewarning of misfortune or death.

"Flip-flops shouldn't be upside down" in Brazil – In Brazil, an overturned flip-flop is thought to bring bad luck or accidents, so it is quickly corrected.

Avoiding clean, wet streets in Thailand – Walking on freshly cleaned streets is believed to bring misfortune or attract negative energy in Thai culture.

Sitting at the corner of a table as unlucky – In Eastern Europe and Russia, sitting at a table's corner is said to doom a person to remain unmarried for seven years.

Section: Rituals That Survive to This Day

Tea ceremony in Japan – This traditional practice reflects harmony, respect, and purity, continuing as an essential expression of Japanese culture and aesthetics.

Burning incense in China – Incense burning in temples and homes is a spiritual tradition aimed at cleansing spaces and connecting with ancestors.

Blessing food on Easter in Poland – The custom of blessing a basket of food on Holy Saturday symbolizes family blessings and prosperity.

Day of the Dead in Mexico – The Día de los Muertos celebration honors the deceased with altars of food and flowers, celebrating their lives.

Fasting during Ramadan – Practiced in Muslim countries, this month-long fast represents spiritual cleansing, humility, and empathy for the needy.

Baptism in Christianity – This water purification ritual symbolizes entry into the religious community and is practiced globally.

Wedding ring exchange – The exchange of rings during weddings symbolizes fidelity and unity, a tradition widespread across cultures worldwide.

New Year's resolutions – The tradition of setting resolutions is a way of reflecting and setting goals for the coming year.

Public baths in Japan – Traditional baths (onsen) remain popular for physical and mental purification, a practice deeply rooted in Japanese culture.

Coptic New Year in Egypt – Known as Neyrouz, this celebration honors martyrs and renews faith.

Blessing rituals in India – During weddings and significant events, elders bless the younger generation to ensure happiness and success.

Throwing rice at newlyweds – A symbol of fertility and prosperity, throwing rice at weddings is practiced in many cultures, including in Asia and Europe.

Tying strings around wrists in Thailand – Called "Sai Sin," white strings tied around wrists symbolize protection and blessings, common during births, weddings, and other occasions.

Bar Mitzvah and Bat Mitzvah in Judaism – Coming-of-age ceremonies for boys and girls mark their transition into adulthood and remain vital in synagogue traditions.

Traditional Balinese cremation ceremonies – Cremation rituals purify the soul and prepare it for its next life, according to Hindu beliefs.

Harvest festivals – Celebrations of the harvest, such as Thanksgiving or Dożynki, express gratitude for crops and highlight humanity's bond with nature.

Washing feet on Holy Thursday – A Christian ceremony symbolizing humility and service, performed during Holy Week.

Throwing coins into fountains – Tossing coins into fountains as a wish for luck and prosperity continues as a widespread tourist tradition.

Hindu fire ritual (Aarti) – Aarti, the offering of light, is a cleansing and devotional ceremony practiced in temples and homes.

Christmas tree traditions – Decorating trees, exchanging gifts, and family gatherings are universal Christmas rituals celebrated across cultures.

Section: Everyday Objects

Fork – Though indispensable today, the fork only gained popularity in Europe in the 16th century, previously considered an oddity.

Glasses – Invented in 13th-century Italy, glasses revolutionized daily life by improving vision and extending people's ability to work.

Toilet paper – Introduced for sale in the US in the 19th century, it is now a household staple, whereas previously, people used materials ranging from leaves to newspapers.

Ballpoint pen – Once dominated by fountain pens, the 20th-century invention of the ballpoint pen offered a practical, accessible solution for everyday writing.

Zipper – Invented in 1913, the zipper transformed clothing and bags, enabling quick fastening and unfastening of jackets, apparel, and luggage.

Alarm clock – The first mechanical alarm clocks appeared in the 18th century, evolving into modern electronic and smartphone alarms, essential for morning routines.

Toothpaste and toothbrush – Toothpaste dates back to ancient Egypt, and the modern toothbrush originated in 15th-century China, revolutionizing personal hygiene.

Frying pan – Used for thousands of years, frying pans are among the oldest kitchen tools, now available in materials from cast iron to stainless steel.

Book – Since Gutenberg's invention of the printing press, books have become widely accessible, forming the foundation of education and entertainment.

Refrigerator – A 19th-century invention, the refrigerator transformed food storage, allowing for longer preservation and altering food management habits.

Light bulb – Invented by Edison and his collaborators in the 19th century, the light bulb extended activity after dark and became the cornerstone of electric lighting.

Matches and lighters – From the invention of matches in the 19th century to modern lighters, fire has become readily available for daily needs.

Headphones – Invented in the 20th century, headphones enable private music listening, phone calls, and are integral to modern digital life.

Smartphone – One of the most significant inventions of the 21st century, the smartphone combines the functions of a phone, computer, camera, and many other devices.

Microwave oven – Accidentally invented in the 20th century, the microwave revolutionized quick food heating, becoming essential in everyday meal preparation.

Plastic bag – Invented in the 1960s, plastic bags became ubiquitous, though their use is now shifting toward more eco-friendly alternatives.

Swiss army knife – A multifunctional tool invented in the 19th century, used for daily tasks and outdoor activities, from opening cans to small repairs.

Thermos – The thermos maintains the temperature of liquids and food, making it indispensable for travel and picnics.

Nail file – A small tool for nail care, popular since the 19th century, it has become a staple of everyday hygiene and grooming.

Umbrella – Known since antiquity, the umbrella protects against rain and sun, remaining a practical everyday item, especially in rainy climates.

Section: Human Labor and Other Professions

Farmers and Ranchers – One of the oldest professions in the world, farmers provide food and raw materials that form the backbone of the economy and daily life.

Craftspeople and Blacksmiths – Trades like blacksmithing, pottery, and weaving have long traditions and continue to pass down unique skills and artistry.

Bakers and Pastry Chefs – These professions require precision and expertise, creating essential items like bread and cakes that enrich daily living.

Teachers – Education plays a vital role in society, and teachers shape future generations by imparting knowledge and values.

Miners – Working in challenging conditions, miners extract raw materials like coal and metals that are indispensable to industry and energy production.

Nurses – A cornerstone of healthcare, nurses provide crucial support to patients and aid in their recovery.

Doctors and Surgeons – Specialists who diagnose, treat, and save lives, their skills and knowledge are essential for community health.

Firefighters – Requiring courage and physical fitness, firefighters protect lives, property, and the environment by responding to fires and disasters.

Police Officers and Municipal Guards – Law enforcement professionals maintain public safety and uphold the law, playing a key role in protecting communities.

Scientists and Researchers – Working in labs and universities, scientists push the boundaries of knowledge, discovering new technologies and solutions for humanity.

Engineers – Experts in construction and technology, engineers design and build infrastructure and tools that improve everyday life.

Programmers – They develop software and applications, making technology more accessible and functional for work, entertainment, and communication.

Mechanics and Technicians – Maintaining and repairing vehicles, appliances, and machinery, these professionals ensure the reliability of essential equipment.

Writers and Journalists – Writers create literature, while journalists deliver news, shaping public opinion and contributing to culture.

Taxi Drivers and Professional Drivers – Responsible for transporting people and goods, drivers play a crucial role in supporting the economy and mobility.

Restaurateurs and Waitstaff – Culinary professionals prepare meals and serve customers, providing entertainment and culinary pleasure in everyday life.

Construction Workers and Bricklayers – Their labor builds homes, buildings, and infrastructure, forming the foundation for urban development and societal growth.

Accountants and Financial Analysts – Specialists in managing finances, they assist businesses and individuals in budgeting and investing.

Artists and Designers – Creators in art, design, and fashion significantly influence aesthetics and culture, from architecture to the clothes we wear.

Social Workers – They provide support to individuals in need, helping them navigate challenges such as mental health issues or difficult life circumstances.

Section: Facts About Our Daily Lives

Average sleep duration decreases with age – Children need around 10–12 hours of sleep, while adults typically sleep 7–8 hours, and seniors often require just 6 hours.

The average person spends about 3 hours a day on digital devices – In many countries, time spent on phones and computers continues to rise, impacting lifestyle and health.

People can read about 200 words per minute – The average adult reading speed ranges from 200 to 300 words per minute, but it can be improved with speed-reading techniques.

The average person spends over a year of their life cleaning – Studies show that regular cleaning takes about 1.5 hours per week, adding up to over a year across a lifetime.

We inhale approximately 11,000 liters of air daily – Our lungs work tirelessly to supply oxygen, which is essential for organ function.

Coffee is the most popular beverage in the world after water – More than half of adults globally drink coffee regularly, and it plays a central role in daily routines across cultures.

Most people laugh about 10–20 times a day – Laughter is a natural mechanism that reduces stress and improves mood, contributing positively to health.

Prolonged sitting is compared to smoking – Sitting for extended periods without movement increases the risk of cardiovascular diseases and diabetes, making physical activity crucial.

The average person speaks about 7,000 words daily – While this number varies by personality, speech remains a fundamental form of social communication.

People spend an average of 6 months of their lives waiting at traffic lights – Urban living involves significant time spent in traffic, shaping drivers' daily experiences.

The average walking speed is about 5 km/h – Walking is the simplest form of exercise, and pace varies based on individual fitness and lifestyle.

The average person spends over 2 years of their life watching TV – Television is one of the most popular forms of entertainment and a daily ritual for many.

70% of people wear clothing in neutral colors – Shades like black, gray, and white are favored for their versatility and ease of pairing with other wardrobe items.

The average person carries about 5 keys – Whether for homes, cars, workplaces, or lockers, most people carry multiple keys daily.

Average outdoor time is about 1 hour a day – In developed countries, most people spend the majority of their time indoors, affecting vitamin D levels and well-being.

Humans produce about 1.5 liters of saliva daily – Saliva aids digestion and cleanses the mouth, with production increasing during meals.

The average person consumes over 35 tons of food in their lifetime – This vast quantity of food has a profound impact on our health and the environment.

People spend about 1 hour a day preparing meals – Cooking serves not only as a way to prepare food but also as a popular hobby and a method of relaxation.

Humans frown an average of 30,000 times daily – Facial expressions are crucial for communication, and frowning can be an unconscious reaction to emotions.

Regular physical activity reduces the risk of many diseases by about 50% – Daily activity, even short walks, has a significant positive effect on health and well-being.

Summary of the Book

"True Facts That Sound Like Bull#t" is a collection of the most astonishing and unbelievable facts that sound so improbable, it's hard to believe they're actually true. Spanning ten chapters, the book takes readers on a journey through surprising trivia from various fields—ranging from the animal kingdom and the wonders of the human body to the mysteries of space, the secrets of chemistry, and the peculiar customs and superstitions that have endured to this day.

Each page reveals facts that seem almost absurd but are rooted in truth. From astonishing phenomena and unique natural traits to bizarre human behaviors and groundbreaking scientific discoveries, this book entertains, educates, and provokes thought. It invites readers to uncover hidden truths about the world, proving that what sounds like a myth is often reality.

"True Facts That Sound Like Bull#t" is the perfect read for those who love to be surprised, want to expand their knowledge with shareable trivia, and seek inspiration to view the world from a completely new perspective. It's a book that captivates from the first page to the last, reminding us how much there is still to discover.

www.ingramcontent.com/pod-product-compliance
Lightning Source LLC
LaVergne TN
LVHW012125070526
838202LV00056B/5859